An Illustrated History of

CARDIFF DOCKS

Volume 1

An Illustrated History of

CARDIFF DOCKS

Volume 1:
Bute West and East Docks
and Roath Dock

John Hutton

· MARITIME HERITAGE ·
from
The NOSTALGIA Collection

This work is dedicated to Mr Harold Lloyd, former Chief Engineer for South Wales Ports, East, a retired gentleman and a friend, and also to another friend, a fellow railway photographer and historian, Mr Frank T. Hornby.

© John Hutton 2008

All rights reserved. No part of this publication may be reproduced, stored in a retrieval system or transmitted, in any form or by any means, electronic, mechanical, photocopying, recording or otherwise, without prior permission in writing from Silver Link Publishing Ltd.

First published in 2008

British Library Cataloguing in Publication Data

A catalogue record for this book is available from the British Library.

ISBN 978 1 85794 305 4

Silver Link Publishing Ltd
The Trundle
Ringstead Road
Great Addington
Kettering
Northants NN14 4BW

Tel/Fax: 01536 330588
email: sales@nostalgiacollection.com
Website: www.nostalgiacollection.com

Printed and bound in the
Czech Republic

A Silver Link book
from
The NOSTALGIA *Collection*

Half title The crest of the Cardiff Railway Company. *Author's collection*

Page 2 Ordnance Survey map of 1901, showing the layout of Cardiff Docks at that time, and at the bottom the area that was later to become the Queen Alexandra Dock. These

Ordnance Survey maps provide a wealth of knowledge and memories to a multitude of people, for many different reasons. *Crown copyright*

Below Extract from the *Railway & Travel Monthly Magazine,* April 1911. *C. W. Harris*

BUTE DOCKS, CARDIFF.

DESCRIPTION.

The Bute Docks are **163** acres in extent, and vessels of a carrying capacity of **12,000 tons** and upwards regularly trade there. The Queen Alexandra and Roath are both walled docks, and are connected by an inter-communication passage **WITH NO LOCKS**, and are kept at the same level, with an average depth of water of 35 feet. The Queen Alexandra sea lock is **850 feet in length, 90 feet in breadth**, with a depth of water over the cill of **42 feet** O.S.T. and **32 feet** O.N.T.

IMPORTS.

Very **extensive accommodation** is provided in the shape of **warehouses and transit sheds** for the storage of **Grain, Provisions, etc.** bonded and free. Large provision is also made for stacking **Timber, Deals, Iron Ore, etc.,** together with **Timber ponds 28 acres** in extent with competitive railway communication to all parts. Extensive refrigerating chill room accommodation is also provided for the storage of **Frozen Meat. Fruit, Provisions, etc.** **Cattle Lairs, Slaughter Houses and Chill Rooms** are erected adjacent to the wharf in the deepest water dock. The Bute Docks are fully equipped with cranes worked by **Hydraulic and Electric pressure** lifting up to **70 tons.**

EXPORTS.

Coal and Coke, Patent Fuel, Iron and Steel Rails, Hardware, etc. are the chief exports, and General Cargoes are shipped to all **parts of the world.** Coal being the chief stable export, great attention has been given in providing the **best appliances** for shipping same. Amongst them may be mentioned the **Lewis-Hunter Coaling Cranes**, and **Armstrong's Coal Hoists,** lifting laden wagons **65 feet** above the quay level. Attention may be drawn to the **Lewis Hunter Coaling Cranes,** which are claimed to ship coal with from **5 to 7%** **less breakage** than any other class of appliance. One of the chief features of the Bute Docks is, that in the modern docks **all the appliances are movable,** so that coal can be loaded into three or four hatchways simultaneously, with the result that **6,715 tons** of coal have been shipped into a vessel in 11 hours.

DOCK CHARGES.

These are much below the average of our great ports. Vessels can generally procure an outward cargo to any Port in the World, thus giving the Bute Docks an advantage for Imports, as vessels do not require to change Ports.
The following table shows the growth of the Bute Docks in decennial periods during the past 30 years:—

1880	..	..	..	..	..	..	..	6,291,137	tons.
1890	..	..	..	..	..	..	..	9,217,960	,,
1900	..	..	..	..	..	..	..	10,300,935	,,
1910	..	..	..	..	..	..	..	12,182,195	,,

NOTE.—Cardiff is the natural Port for Birmingham and the Midland District, and the Bute Docks are the only docks situated in the city of Cardiff.

For further information please apply to the Cardiff Railway Co., Cardiff.
C. S. DENNISS, General Manager.

CONTENTS

Painting of the Bute and Roath Docks, Cardiff, circa 1894. *Associated British Ports*

CARDIFF RAILWAY COMPANY.

Bute Docks, Cardiff.

Chairman	-	LORD EDMUND TALBOT, M.P.
Managing Director	-	SIR WILLIAM THOMAS LEWIS, BART.
Superintendent	-	JAMES HURMAN.

AREA, ETC. The present **BUTE DOCKS** are 111 acres in extent, and vessels loading up to 12,000 tons regularly trade there.

THE **NEW SOUTH DOCK**, which is rapidly approaching completion, will have a water area of 50 acres. It is 2,550 ft. in length, 800 ft. in breadth, and 50 ft. in depth from the coping; and will be capable of accommodating the **LARGEST VESSELS AFLOAT.** The Sea Lock will be 850 feet in length, and 90 feet in breadth, with a depth of water over the cill of 42 ft. at ordinary spring tides, and 32 ft. at ordinary neap tides. Two Large Graving Docks, up to 850 feet in length, and entered from this Dock, are about to be constructed.

MACHINERY AND APPLIANCES. The Bute Docks are equipped with the **MOST IMPROVED APPLIANCES** for the discharging and loading of Vessels with dispatch; the greater portion being worked by HYDRAULIC PRESSURE. There is an ample equipment of Cranes of various power up to 70 tons, as well as **Grain Elevators**, &c., &c.

Special attention may be drawn to the **NEW 70-TON CRANE** in the **ROATH DOCK,** thus enabling **THE CARDIFF RAILWAY COMPANY** to ship or unship **THE HEAVIEST WEIGHTS.**

COAL SHIPPING FACILITIES. Coal is being shipped at these Docks by the ordinary Fixed, as well as Movable Staiths; as also by the **LEWIS-HUNTER PATENT COALING CRANES.**

The Cardiff Railway Company have the exclusive use in the Bristol Channel of the **Lewis-Hunter** Coaling Cranes, which have proved by far the most satisfactory appliances for shipping Welsh Coal with dispatch and the **Least Possible Breakage.** Colliery screened coal shipped by these Cranes being equal to double screened coal shipped by ordinary Staiths, and thereby ensuring to the purchaser an increased value of at least **One Shilling** per ton over that of coal put on board by shipping appliances at other Docks, besides ensuring great saving in breakage and uniformity of distribution throughout the cargo of any small coal that might exist; thus minimising any risk of spontaneous ignition from small coal in cargoes bound for distant ports. **THREE OR MORE CRANES** can be worked simultaneously into one vessel, and as much as **330 tons** have been shipped by one crane in an hour, and **6,715 tons** have been shipped into a vessel in **11 hours.** Shippers attach so much importance to the advantages of these Cranes that they frequently elect to wait some time for a **Crane Berth** rather than have their coal shipped by the usual staiths.

THE NEW SOUTH DOCK will be entirely equipped with these Coaling Cranes, in deference to the wishes of so many Shippers and Buyers of **CARDIFF COAL.**

WAREHOUSES AND TRANSIT SHEDS. Good accommodation for the storage of **GRAIN, PROVISIONS,** &c., &c., **BONDED AND FREE.**

WHARF SPACE AND YARDS. Large provision is made for stacking Timber, Deals, Iron Ore, &c. Timber Ponds. 28 ACRES in extent, with COMPETITIVE RAILWAY COMMUNICATION TO ALL PARTS.

FACILITIES FOR SHIP REPAIRS, ETC. There are 10 **PRIVATE GRAVING AND FLOATING DOCKS,** ranging up to 800 ft. in length, with **SEPARATE PROPRIETARIES,** and one **PUBLIC GRAVING DOCK,** 600 ft. in length. There are also several **MARINE ENGINEERING FIRMS,** thus giving Shipowners an opportunity of obtaining tenders for repairs of every description.

RAILWAY ACCOMMODATION. **CARDIFF** is the **NATURAL PORT** for **BIRMINGHAM** and the **MIDLAND DISTRICT,** as the London & North Western, Midland, and Great Western Railway Companies have direct communication from the Ship's Side.

DOCK CHARGES. These are much below the average of our Great Ports. Vessels can generally procure an outward cargo to any Port in the World, thus giving Bute Docks an advantage for Imports, as vessels do not require to change Ports.

TRADE. The **BUTE DOCKS** were opened in the year **1839,** and the **IMPORTS** and **EXPORTS** in **1904** were as follows: Imports, 2,020,936 tons; Exports, 8,250,082 tons; TOTAL, **10,271,018** tons.

CATTLE IMPORTATION.—The **BUTE DOCKS** are the **ONLY DOCKS** in South Wales which have permission from the BOARD OF TRADE to land FOREIGN CATTLE. Excellent Cattle Lairs, Slaughter Houses, and Chill Rooms are erected adjacent to the Wharf in the deepest-water dock, with Railways leading into them, having communication with all parts.

COLD STORAGE.—Ample Accommodation of the most modern description is provided for the storage of dead meat, poultry, provisions, vegetables, &c.

STATUS OF CARDIFF. **CARDIFF** now occupies the position of being the **FIRST PORT** in the **UNITED KINGDOM** for shipping cleared to Foreign Countries and British Possessions, and the **PREMIER PORT** in the **WORLD** for the **SHIPMENT OF COAL.**

NOTE.— The Bute Docks are the only Docks situated in the Town of Cardiff. Vessels using the Bute Docks thereby save their owners and Captains from loss of time in making journeys between the Vessels and the Merchants' and Brokers' Offices, Banks, Custom House, Post Office, &c., all of which Offices are adjacent to the Bute Docks.

The fullest information on all matters will be readily granted on application to—

THE CARDIFF RAILWAY COMPANY,
Bute Docks, CARDIFF.

Advertisement by the Cardiff Railway Company in *The Maritime Review*, 4 August 1905. *Author's collection*

FOREWORD

by Callum Couper, Port Manager, Associated British Ports, Cardiff and Barry

Much has been published about the history of Cardiff and its port, once known throughout the world for the Rhondda steam coal that passed over its quays, shipped worldwide to fuel the global expansion of industry, trade and economic power during the latter half of the 19th century.

In these three volumes John Hutton has added to this literature, superbly capturing Cardiff's remarkable maritime history with many hundreds of photographs, maps and ephemera, each richly annotated to provide historical detail and provenance.

The author's meticulous work comes from archive material held by the Port and other companies, public records and first-hand interviews with people who have traded or worked in Cardiff's docklands. He traces the port from its earliest known beginnings through the Industrial Revolution, World Wars and into the present day.

The physical development of Cardiff's docks, demanding the most innovative civil engineering works on a huge scale, was spectacular, and the port's cargo trade grew year on year from the late 1830s to its zenith during the prosperous Edwardian years at the eve of the First World War.

Cardiff's Roman fort, the remains of which can still be seen, demonstrates how long the sheltered waters of the River Taff have provided a place at which to land cargo and people. However, it was during the late 18th century that the port began in earnest to serve the mineral-rich valleys of South Wales with their rapidly expanding industries and iron foundries all seeking a reliable and cost-effective market for their products.

The Glamorganshire Canal, which opened in February 1794, was the first impounded waterway to provide a route to the sea at Cardiff. Within 45 years of the canal's opening, the first true dock, Bute West, was opened for shipping. Over the next 68 years, between 1839 and 1907, an interconnected dock system, rivalling that of any other port in the world, was constructed, comprising 17 docks, dock basins and dry docks, 165 acres of water and 7 miles of linear quay, excluding the neighbouring Penarth Dock and Glamorganshire Canal facilities. At its peak in 1913 Cardiff handled a total of 13,676,941 imperial tons of exports and imports, the greater part being 'black gold' mined from the South Wales Coalfield.

In 2007 the last of the docks to be constructed, the Queen Alexandra Dock, celebrated its centenary, which was marked by an open day for the community involving exhibitions and waterborne tours of the docks system. While the old Bute West and East docks are no longer extant, and the Roath Basin is now given over to leisure uses and has become the centre point of the very successful 'Cardiff Bay' regeneration, the remaining commercial docks continue to prosper with new investment supporting new trades, without a dram of coal in sight!

The Queen Alexandra and Roath docks today comprise some 84 acres of water enclosed by 2.7 miles of linear quay, and in 2007 between them they handled 3 million tonnes of cargo. Cardiff is now a modern regional port with a deep hinterland extending into the Midlands, the South West and the M4 corridor. A broad spread of trade and ongoing capital investment in new port facilities made by its owners, Associated British Ports, ensures that Cardiff continues to be a major player in the UK's maritime trade.

John Hutton's many hours of meticulous research have produced an absorbing work for all those interested in the history of Cardiff and its role during a period of world trade and industrialisation that changed our patterns of life for ever, and he is to be congratulated for his fine pictorial history of the Port of Cardiff.

Callum Couper
January 2008

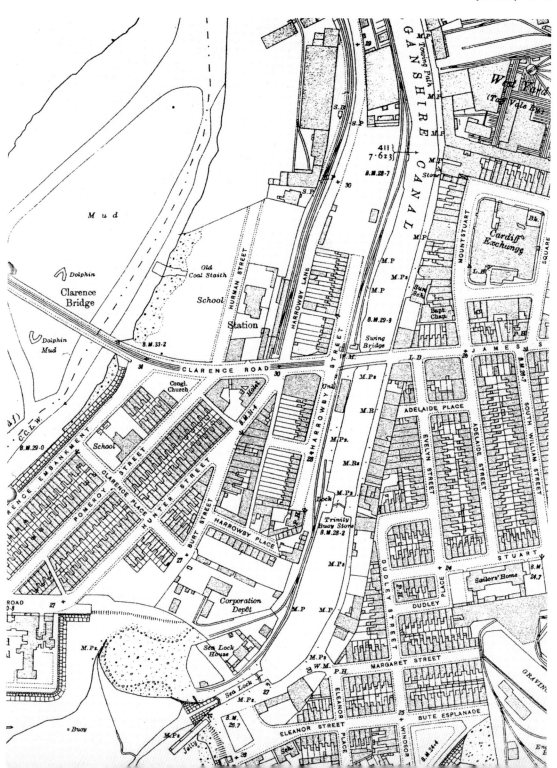

INTRODUCTION

As long ago as 589 AD the Port of Cardiff was defined as reaching from Chepstow to Worms Head. Perhaps this was a bit of an exaggeration, but the first recognised berth for the loading and discharging of cargo was a quay said to have been constructed in 1263, situated at the junction of the River Taff and the Tanyard Brook. During this period some private wharves were located below the town quay, and in 1560, and again in 1685, a small quantity of coal is recorded as having been shipped to the French ports of Rochelle and Bordeaux. By 1685 the Port of Cardiff was defined as stretching from the River Wye to Worms Head, but trade to and from this small port was not great – at least, not by any modern standard.

Flowing between Cardiff and Bristol was the Severn Estuary, which for seamen was treacherous water, with the captains of merchant vessels having very little in the way of landmarks to guide them into safe anchorage at the few river wharves that were surrounded by mud at low tide. If you crept up the estuary in a good light on a high tide it was possible to spot one of the few landmarks; for example, in 1777 it was recorded that one could sight the haystack at Adams Farm in the village of Adamstown – if you were lucky, and the weather conditions were in your favour, with no driving rain stinging your face and hands, or snow that froze your body and jammed the ropes in their pulley blocks, or a thick river fog that slowed your pace down to less than a knot, while you strained your eyes and, more importantly, ears for the dreaded sound of water crashing against rocks. It was no small wonder that the Customs Collector

of Cardiff wrote in his report of 1782 that he predicted that no coal would ever be exported from Cardiff. However, some eight years later, on 9 June 1790, Royal Assent was given by His Majesty King George III to the Glamorgan Canal Act, for the making of a canal from Abercynon to Cardiff (the extension from Abercynon to Aberdare was not opened for traffic until 1811).

The making of this canal was a task that was not without hardship, difficulties and danger, involving accidents and deaths. Not only did the canal itself have to be made, but also the wharves, lock gates and keepers' cottages that would ensure the smooth running of the goods and mineral traffic. Dram roads had to be made to the collieries, iron foundries and the many other smaller concerns that were located nearby, for iron and coal would be the main products to be transported along the 25 miles of waterway; up to 20 tons could be carried on one barge.

In February 1794 the Glamorganshire Canal opened to traffic, joining Merthyr Tydfil with the Port of Cardiff. In the same year an Act was passed to authorise completion of the canal, including the construction of a sea lock separating the canal from the waters of the Channel. This lock was completed in 1798, and land on either side of it was let out for wharves or coal yards; by 1839 11 coal yards, one bark yard, 13 wharves, two dry docks, three warehouses and two lumber yards were in operation, allowing vessels of up to 200 tons (gross registered tonnage, reduced to 100 in the dry summer months) to make direct use of the canal by transhipping direct from barge to ship. In addition, two coaling staiths were erected on the bank of the River Taff, where the course of the river was close to the basin on the east side, for the loading of small coasters during high tide.

By 1820 some 50,000 tons of iron and coal had been carried down the canal, within ten years the figure had risen to 200,000 tons, and by 1839 it

Left Ordnance Survey map of 1920, showing the Glamorganshire Canal and its Sea Lock, as well as the many houses that had sprung up with the prosperity that the canal and docks had brought to the area. On 5 December 1951 the Sea Lock gates were destroyed by contact with a sand dredger, and the water escaped. *Crown copyright*

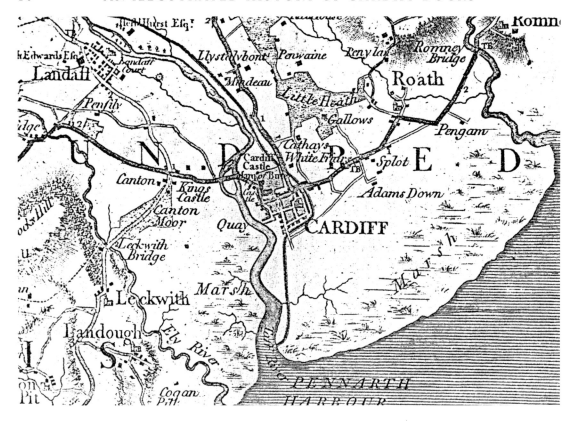

Above Yates's map of the County of South Glamorgan, circa 1799. The Glamorganshire
Canal can be plainly seen, winding its way down to the estuary of the River Taff. *Author's collection*

was 350,000 tons. The port was expanding, and the merchants were sharing in the prosperity that the canal had brought. Certainly the future for Cardiff had arrived, but there still was a long way to go. The wharf facilities could no longer cope with the amount of traffic. This area of Cardiff was still predominantly agricultural land, and sheep grazed on the nearby Pontcanna fields, although some land had been used for buildings, warehouses and dwellings. Space was at a premium, and there were other problems that also did not help: during the winter months the water in the upper section of the canal froze over, holding barges, and lock gates, in a grip of ice, while in a dry summer another drawback was a scarcity of water.

Two ideas were born from these failings. The first was a railway from Merthyr Tydfil to Cardiff, and the second the building of a new dock to handle the ever-increasing volume of traffic. Thus it was on 16 July 1830 that the Bute Ship Canal Act was passed, giving John, 2nd Marquis of Bute (1793-1848), the power to construct a new dock, entirely at his own expense and risk. It took another six years of deliberation before the site for his new dock was selected, and construction commenced in 1837. It must be noted that in locating his dock in Cardiff, at the mouth of the River Taff and at a point where the Glamorganshire Canal reached the Bristol Channel, the Marquis had made a shrewd choice that would guarantee a large share of all manner of traffic that came down from the valleys. In the early years this was mainly iron from Dowlais and Merthyr; however, by 1913 almost all of the traffic passing through the docks was coal.

Left This engraving, looking from the remains of Cardiff Castle ramparts, shows a scene that combines activity with industry. On the left is the tower of St John's Church, with the old High Street Town Hall near the centre, and beyond a panoramic view overlooking the town looking south towards the Tidal Basin, with the Glamorganshire Canal entrance in the distance behind the Town Hall. Also visible are the kilns and chimneys of Messrs J. J. Guest's glassworks, which would eventually mark the terminus of the Taff Vale Railway. In the far distance are the islands of Flat Holm and Steep Holm (a touch of artistic licence, perhaps). The picture was drawn by W. H. Bartlett (1809-54) and engraved by J. H. Lekeux (1783-1846). The date is given as circa 1841, but there is no sign of the Taff Vale Railway, so maybe it is a little earlier, perhaps 1836. Cardiff Central Library, Local Studies Department

A channel or feeder had to be cut at a point some 2 miles above the mouth of the river to supply the newly built dock with water, then, on 9 October 1839, the first vessel, The Lady Charlotte, entered the Bute West Dock. The Marquis of Bute had an agreement with the Taff Vale Railway that, on completion, his dock would handle all of that company's mineral traffic from Merthyr Tydfil. Later came the Bute East Dock, built and enlarged between 1852 and 1859; dock lines owned by the company were also built, both to serve the new dock and link it with the lines of the Bute West Dock. In addition, the Rhymney Railway and the broad gauge Great Western Railway built lines into the East Dock, so by the time both docks were fully operational coal traffic alone had amounted to more than 2 million tons per year.

The Bute Docks were so successful that from 1880 onwards only a small quantity of domestic coal came down the old canal system, the principal traffic being patent fuel from the Maindy Works, but even that traffic ceased with the closure of the works in 1928, and by 1941 most of the neglected canal had been filled in.

The continued growth of traffic arriving at the docks became instrumental in the encouragement of the building of the Roath Basin in 1869, followed by the Roath Dock in 1887. Under the Bute Docks Transfer Act of 25 June 1886 the Bute Docks Company was incorporated, formed to take over from the Bute Trustees, which had been formed on 20 February 1845 and re-established under the Bute Estates Act of 31 August 1848. The new company consisted of directors drawn from the Trustees.

The short extension of the GWR branch to the Roath Basin, opened on 17 January 1854, was converted from broad gauge to standard gauge in 1872. Meanwhile, the machinery for handling the coal traffic was being improved, giving the docks ever-increasing handling facilities. In 1897 the Cardiff Railway Company was incorporated.

On 13 July 1907 Their Majesties King Edward VII and Queen Alexandra opened the Queen Alexandra Dock, which, with its sea lock entrance, would be the largest, made necessary by the ever-increasing coal export trade.

A further Royal visit was paid to the docks on 27 June 1912, when Their Majesties King George V and Queen Mary toured the Taff, Rhondda and

THE Bute Docks of the Cardiff Railway, under the able superintendence of Mr. James Hurman, are enjoying a most encouraging period of prosperity. The figures for 1907 establish a record both in the volume of general trade and in coal export shipments. The previous record year for general trade, was 1899, when the total import and export trade from the Bute Docks amounted to 10,957,793 tons, and it was in that year also that the record of coal and coke exports was also established, with shipments, amounting to 8,279,005 tons, but the figures in both these cases were exceeded in 1907, when the aggregate imports and exports totalled nearly 12,000,000 tons. A new dock, it will be remembered, was opened on July 18th last, by H.M. the King, and it has been found necessary to promote a Bill in the present Session of Parliament for authorising some short lines of railway in connection with the new dock, and for certain extensions of time for completion of works.

Extract from *The Railway Magazine*, August 1908.

Aberdare Valleys before returning to the Royal Yacht moored in the Queen Alexandra Dock.

As well as the coal export trade, the docks also handled imported cattle and livestock, using cattle lairs that contained chill rooms and an abattoir. Other principal imports were timber from Scandinavia and Russia, and iron ore for the new East Moors Steelworks.

In 1922 these privately owned docks and their railway were amalgamated with other existing Great Western Railway-owned docks under the management of the newly formed GWR Docks Department, administered by the Chief Docks Manager, with headquarters in the Pierhead Building at Cardiff Bute Docks. In 1927 the administration of the GWR-owned cross-channel steamers serving Ireland and the Channel Islands were transferred from the Marine Department at Fishguard to the Docks Department at Cardiff.

Under the Transport Act of 1947 what had by then become the four principal British railway companies – the GWR, LMS, LNER and SR, formed by the 'Grouping' of 1922/23 – would on 1 January 1948 become the nationalised British Railways. Then, on 1 August 1948 the ports of South Wales were transferred to the newly formed Docks & Inland Waterways Executive, becoming part of the British Transport Commission in 1955. In 1963 they became part of the British Transport Docks Board, and in 1964 the decision was taken to withdraw all coal-shipping facilities from Cardiff and Newport and transfer them to Barry

Docks. That same year Bute West Dock was closed, followed by Bute East Dock on 31 January 1970. In 1978 iron ore imported for the East Moors Steelworks in Cardiff Docks ceased following closure by the British Steel Corporation. In 1982 the former British Transport Docks Board was reconstituted as Associated British Ports, under the provisions of the Transport Act 1981.

Associated British Ports' annual booklet, *Port of Cardiff*, 2003 edition, described the docks thus:

The Port of Cardiff is situated on the north side of the Bristol Channel, at the mouth of the River Taff. The westerly position of the port gives sheltered accommodation for suitable vessels of up to 35,000 dwt [deadweight tonnage] and is perfectly placed for traffic to and from the Iberian Peninsula, the Mediterranean, North and West Africa, North and South America, and the Far East. There is a direct road link to the M4 via the A48(M), most berths at the port are rail-connected and there is a daily EWS 'Enterprise' [rail] service operating out of the port.

Facilities
The port has eight general cargo berths with transit shed accommodation of 32,810 square metres, and back shed accommodation of 13,870 square metres. There are 14 open storage berths backed by a total of 26 hectares of storage space. All the general cargo berths and a number of the open berths are equipped with quayside cranes with varying capacities of up to 15 tonnes. Other specialist facilities include three oil terminals, a waste oil treatment plant, a cool store suitable for storing fruit and vegetables, and a cold store with a capacity for approximately 9,000 pallets, which is able to operate with temperatures down to -29 degrees C. There is also a container terminal operated by the Coastal Container Line.

Traffic
The port is renowned for its versatility and ability to handle almost any type of traffic quickly and efficiently from such bulk traffics as scrap metal, woodchips, aggregates, and a variety of minerals to conventional traffics

such as timber, plywood, wood pulp, steel, fruit and vegetables.

Berths

General cargo: 12; scrap: 1; aggregates: 4; oil: 3.

Storage: 5 transit sheds (32,810 square metres); 2 back sheds (13,870 square metres); open storage: 26 hectares; cold store: 9,000 tonnes.

Equipment: Quay cranes: 1 at 15 tonnes capacity, 8 at 7½ tonnes capacity. Container cranes: 2 at 30 tonnes capacity. Forklift trucks: the port provides a fleet of forklift trucks for quayside cargo handling ranging from 4,000 to 8,000lb, including a full range of accessories to handle drums, reels, bales, containers, etc. Mobile crane: 1 at 160 tonnes capacity. Overhead gantry cranes: 6 at 10 tonnes capacity.

Throughout these books, as we slowly move through the history of Cardiff Docks, many maps and photographs are included, showing the changes over the years that would have been witnessed by vessels trading here, and the many and varied buildings and sights that would have been fascinating to behold. Yet at best it is only a glimpse of a way of life that has all but gone, together with the smell of hot steam mixed with oil, the taste of coal dust in your mouth, the clang of loose-coupled wagons being shunted, the shouting and curses of men as they carried heavy sacks of grain or manhandled awkward and heavy barrels and all the huge variety of cargo that passed through the warehouses. We also witness the skills of the administration staff, with countless letters, telegrams, local and international telephone calls, now all replaced by the world of technology and computers, and the different, and perhaps more demanding, workforce now needed for the handling of the daily imports and exports that constantly pass through the docks today.

Yet while the illustrations remind us of the past, and of how things were, I also feel that the modern docks are progressing towards a brighter future, and that the people who work here today, like the men and women of yesteryear, still demonstrate a comradeship, a unique sense of humour, and a pride that still shows through, just as much as it did in the past.

I hope therefore, that you enjoy the journey, for it is timeless.

John Hutton
2008

Steamers discharging pitwood at Bute East Dock in July 1908. A number of pitwood lengths can be seen stacked upright, helping to raise the level of wood carried in the wagons to well above the height of the sides, giving maximum profit per journey. *The Railway Magazine, July 1908*

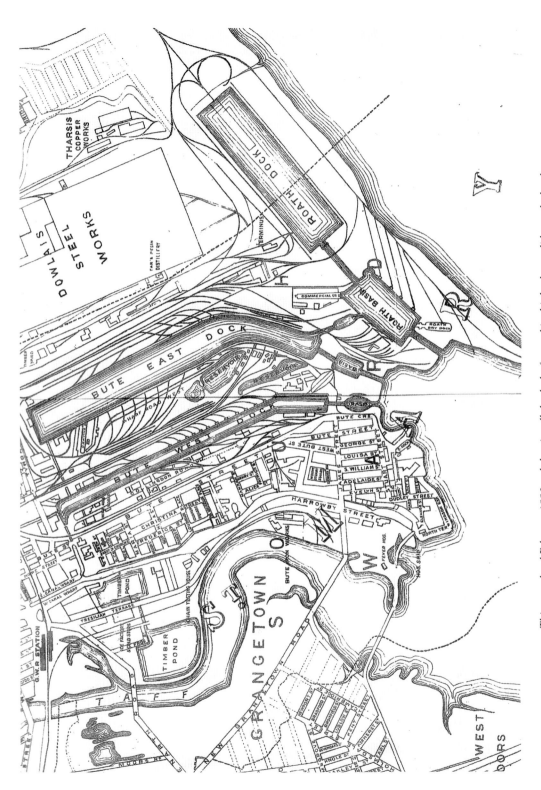

This map, dated February 1890 and showing all the docks featured in this book, was lithographed and published by William Lewis, Ordnance Survey Department, 22 Duke Street, Cardiff. *A. G. Powell*

1. BUTE WEST DOCK

The dock and its basin were officially opened on 9 October 1839 as the Bute Ship Canal, being renamed Bute West Dock on 20 July 1855. The dock was leased by the Marquis of Bute to the Taff Vale Railway Company, which used it from 1841. The TVR feeder lines ran along the east side of the dock, and later to the west side of East Dock. The West Dock was 4,000 feet long by 200 feet wide and covered an area of 18 acres (some reports say 19), with a quayage of 8,800 feet in 1882. In 1913 there were 13 loading staiths and seven cranes in this dock.

Right A County of Glamorgan map showing the 'Bute Ship Canal' and the Taff Vale Railway serving it, and the Glamorganshire canal, circa 1841. *Author's collection*

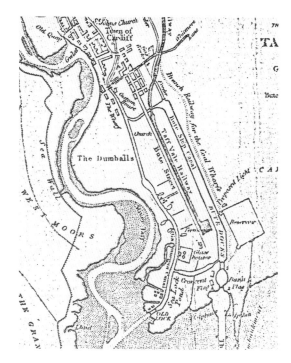

Below Plan showing the 'proposed mode of the laying of the ground near the Bute Ship Dock for various wharfs' to be used for the coal and iron trade. Note on the left the proposed site for the Taff Vale Railway Station, fronted by a Public Wharf. Dated 1840, the plan is signed by Robert Stephenson, the talented son of George. *Associated British Ports*

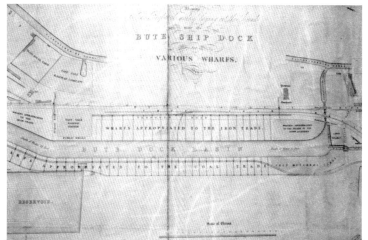

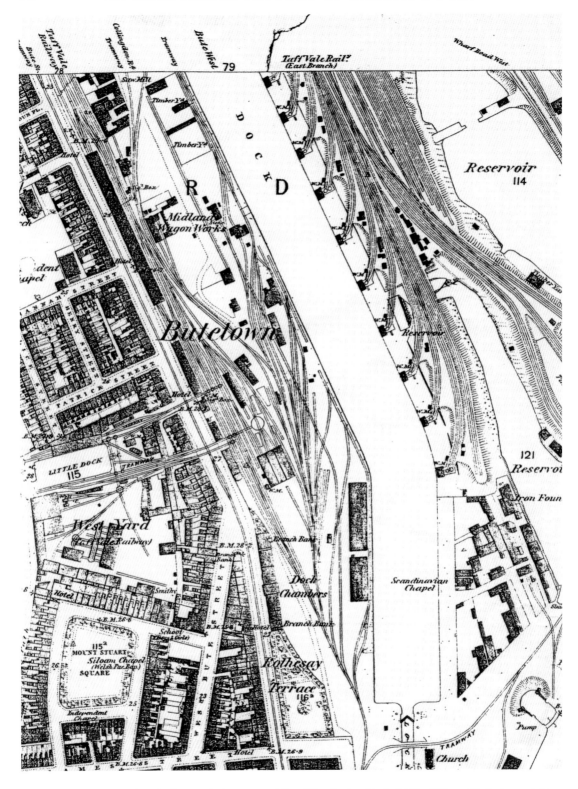

Ordnance Survey map of 1882, showing the lower part of Bute West Dock, with the Midland Wagon Works (upper left), the TVR's West Yard Works (lower left), the Scandinavian Chapel (lower right), and much more. *Crown copyright*

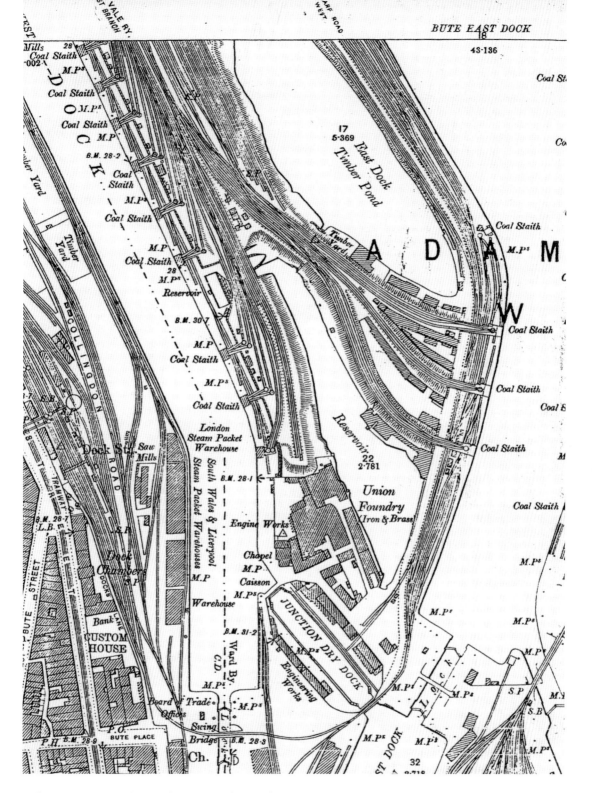

Ordnance Survey map of 1901, showing a similar area, but now with the addition of Junction Dry Dock (bottom), and some of the coal staiths feeding the west side of Bute East Dock. Plainly seen again are some of the numerous coaling staiths erected to give the Taff Vale Railway access to vessels moored along the east side of West Dock. Also of interest is the large area covered by the East Dock Timber Pond, with a convenient timber yard alongside. *Crown copyright*

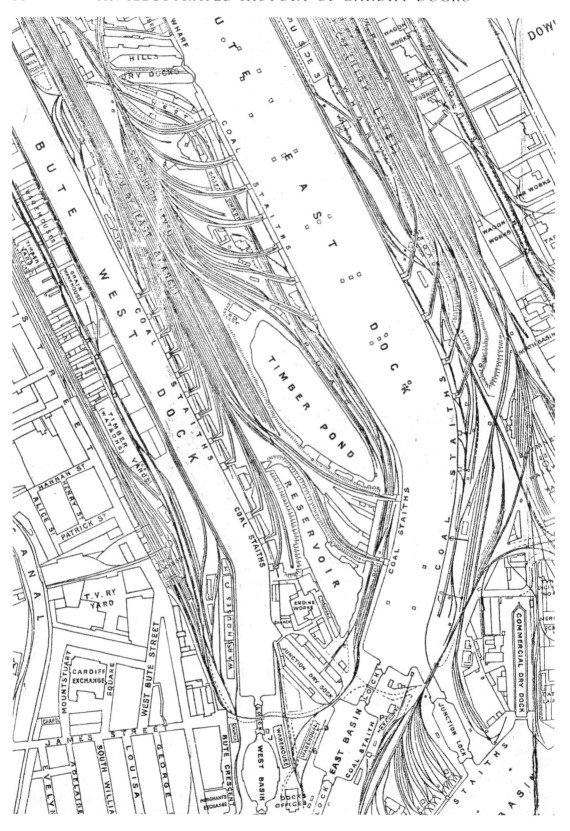

Left Cardiff Railway Company map of 1913, showing Bute West and East Docks, warehouses, buildings and surrounding streets. *Author's collection*

Above This aerial view, circa 1923, gives a clear view of the docks, especially the Bute West Dock and its basin. The centrepiece in the foreground is the Pierhead Building, which was the Cardiff Docks Company offices. To the left in the basin is a floating crane dredging silt and loading the dumb barge alongside. Two ships are moored together beside the South Wales & Liverpool Steam Packet warehouses at the bend on the left of the dock, and opposite them tramp steamers and colliers are taking on coal from the high-level staiths. To their right is the previously mentioned timber pond, and beyond that can be seen Bute East Dock, north of which is the large area covered by the Dowlais (Cardiff) Steelworks. Between the works and the timber pond is a hydraulic pumping station, whose high chimneys could be seen for miles. South of the timber pond can be seen the Junction Dry Dock, with the Scandinavian Chapel at its northern entrance. Between this and the rear of the Pierhead Building can be seen scaffolding in place during the construction of buildings for Messrs Kerman, general engineering merchants. The photograph illustrates very well the vast area of land covered by the docks, as well as providing a feel for the atmosphere of the place. *Associated British Ports*

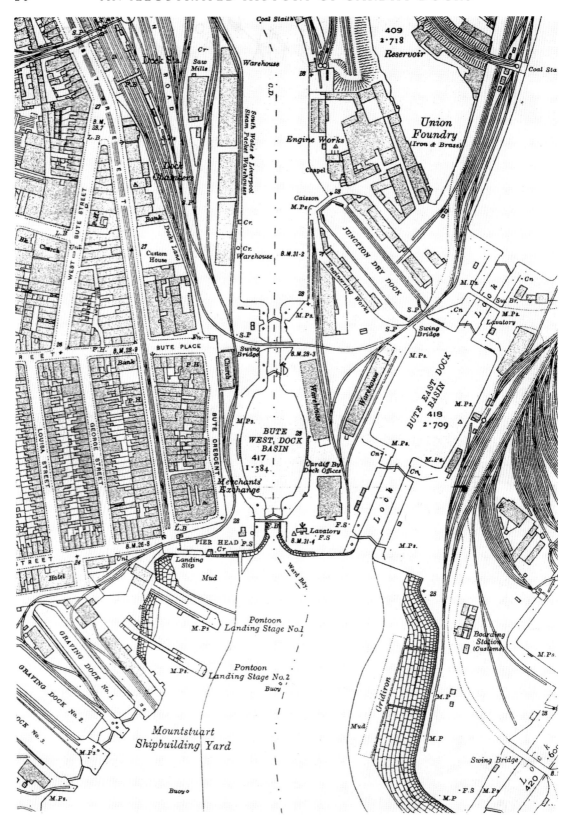

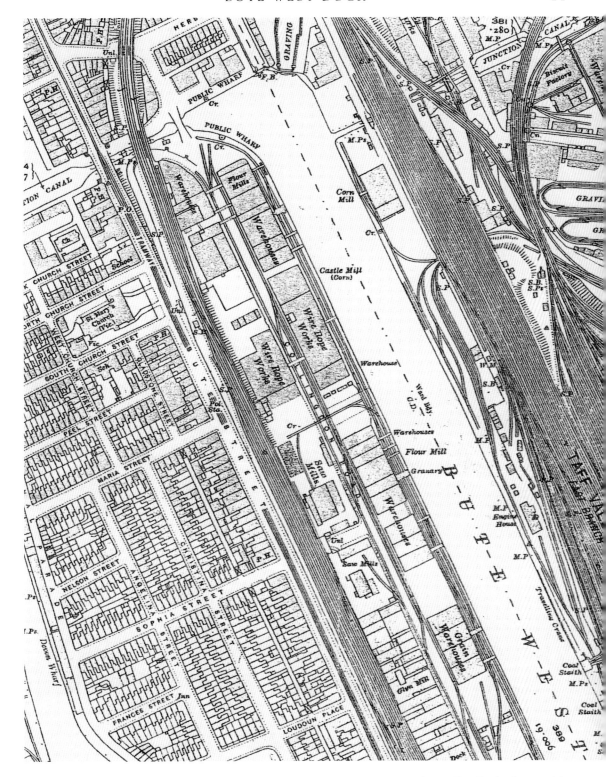

Left Ordnance Survey map of 1920, giving a good indication of the general layout of the entrance channels into the Bute West and East docks. *Crown copyright*

Above The upper part of Bute West Dock, also in 1920. *Crown copyright*

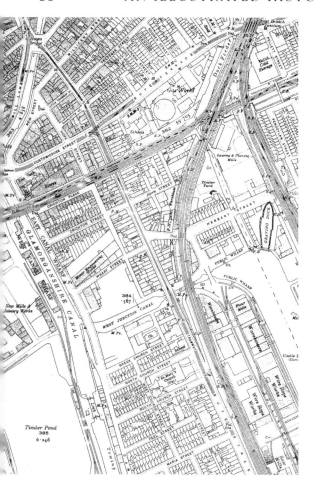

Left Another section from the 1920 Ordnance Survey map, showing the Glamorganshire Canal and top end of Bute West Dock, with its Public Wharfs and the nearby West Junction Canal, feeding the dock from the canal. The Taff Vale Railway's West and East branches are also plainly in view, as they cross the main GWR South Wales main line en route to the docks. *Crown copyright*

Below This aerial view, taken on 6 August 1930, gives a clear view of the complexity of the railways that fed the ever-hungry coaling tips of Bute West and East Docks. On the left are the houses of Butetown, and on the right of Bute Street are the Taff Vale Railway's lines; on the extreme left is the platform of the TVR terminus, by now known as Bute Road station. A line of buildings separate the busy tracks from Collingdon Road, beyond which in turn are a mixture of waterfront buildings, warehouses and flour mills. What is immediately obvious is the large area of water in Bute East Dock – the lessons of congestion had been well learned when it was built, although over time even this dock became too small. The power house and its associated chimney, which supplied hydraulic power to this area of the docks, can be clearly seen in the centre of the photograph. *Associated British Ports*

Bute West Dock Basin

The Entrance Lock was 300 feet in length by 45 feet wide, and the Basin itself was 300 feet long by 200 feet wide, covering an area of 1½ acres. The Inner Lock was 152 feet long by 36 feet wide.

Bute West Dock Basin Entrance Lock consisted of a single pair of gates crossed by a walkway, which was handy for dockers to reach the east side, especially for the 'white collar' workers walking to the dock offices at the nearby Pierhead Building of 1893. The West Dock Basin, or Oval Basin as it was also known, had no cranes or staiths shown on the map of 1882. On the west side of the basin was what became known as the Mission to Seamen Church, a substantial building that opened in 1891 and survived until the very end.

The passage from the basin into Bute West Dock was via the Inner Lock. Between the inner and outer pairs of gates was a swing bridge that carried railway and pedestrian traffic from the Taff Vale Railway's Dock station, in Bute Street, to the west side of East Dock; this line also crossed over the Junction Dry Dock, which lay between the East Dock Basin and the West Dock. The *GWR Magazine* of 1932 recorded that a new double-track swing bridge had been built to carry railway and road traffic across the lock, to replace an old single-track bridge.

On the 1882 Ordnance Survey map (page 16), next to the swing bridge on the east side of the lock was a church, but by 1901 this has gone, replaced by a warehouse, later known as 'J' Warehouse. This was a corrugated-iron building with one floor, 232 feet long by 50 feet wide, used for the storage of general goods. Also seen on the 1882 map is a small park located below the Dock Chambers, shown as Rothesay Terrace; by 1901 this has also gone, replaced by the Custom House and Board of Trade offices in Bute Place. At right-angles, parallel with the basin, is Bute Crescent, at the south end of which was the Merchants Exchange building. By 1977 all the buildings in Bute Crescent had been demolished and replaced by the Welsh Industrial & Maritime Museum, which opened on 15 April of that year. The map of 1982 shows that the Bute West Basin and its lock have been filled in, and a new road, Junction Lock Road, now passes over the site on the same alignment as the railway that crossed the Inner Lock swing bridge, to join up with James Street.

A coloured sketch, dated 1840, showing the design by Robert Stephenson, assisted by George Turnbull, for the entrance to the Bute Ship Canal, showing an elevation of the sea gates and wing walls. *Associated British Ports*

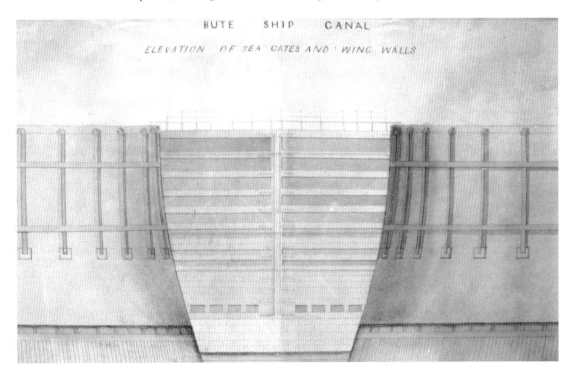

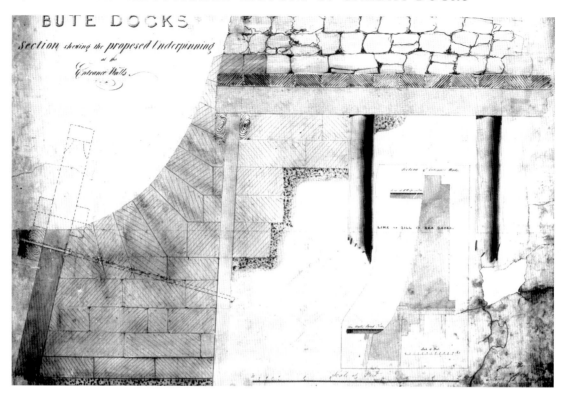

Above and below Sketches showing the plan for the proposed underpinning of the entrance walls of the Bute West Dock, circa 1840-47. *Associated British Ports*

Left Robert Stephenson's signature on one of the 1840 plans for the new dock. *Associated British Ports*

This undated photograph, taken from the east side of Bute West Dock Basin – also known as the Oval Basin because of its shape – shows just how busy the place was. The buildings in the background front on to Bute Street, and were generally occupied by those involved in the shipping business. In the bottom right-hand corner is the vessel *Victor*, registered in Arbroath, and on the far side is another registered in Newcastle. Beyond are two fishing trawlers of the firm of Messrs Neale and West. *Associated British Ports*

This similar view shows a very crowded West Dock Basin, photographed from a window in the Pierhead Building in about 1935. In the distance can clearly be seen the Mission for Seamen Church. Near the camera is a tug with its tow-line stretched to its limit, waiting to enter West Dock in this very busy scene. *Associated British Ports*

The Mission to Seamen Church, on the west side of Bute West Dock Basin, is seen here in about 1930, with Bute Street behind. *Associated British Ports*

This view shows the sea wall between Bute West Dock Basin entrance and the bottom of Bute Street. The large building is Powell Duffryn House, occupied by William Cory & Son Ltd, shipping agents; this grand building was constructed in 1902 on the site of the former Merchants Exchange, which had burned down in 1892. *Cardiff Central Library, Local Studies Department*

This is the east side of Bute West Dock Basin looking south in about 1910, with carts loaded with potatoes. This general wharf was the location of Messrs England's Potato Wharf, and the potatoes were mostly handled using female labour. This very interesting scene contains horse-drawn carts, baskets and sacks, and men standing alongside their carts awaiting their turn to load up. On the far left are the dock offices. *Associated British Ports*

In about 1905 we are looking from the Basin towards West Dock. Nearest the camera is a collection of dumb barges, which would have to be towed to their destination by a powered barge, then roped alongside a vessel to receive or discharge cargo. Usually they would carry a variety of goods, and at this period it is fair to assume that they would use the Glamorganshire Canal, whose sea lock is only a short distance from the West Dock Basin entrance. The barges appear to be carrying briquettes of patent fuel, perhaps from the Maindy Star Works. *Associated British Ports*

Right In December 1964 *Ship Ahoy* magazine reported that a number of tugs owned by C. J. King & Co (Tugs) Ltd, of Avonmouth, had made appearances on the north side of the channel, including the steam tugs *Bristolian* (1911, 174gt) and *Sea Alarm* (1941, 263gt). Here *Sea Alarm* is seen in the by then closed Bute West Dock Basin in about 1977. Built at Sunderland by John Crown & Sons Ltd for the Ministry of War Transport, she was registered at Glasgow by the Clyde Shipping Company, acting as managers for the Ministry. Her length was 107ft 8in, breadth 26ft 2in, and draught 12ft 5in, and she was fitted with a triple-expansion steam engine with cylinders of 16½, 27 and 46 inches, and a stroke of 30 inches, producing 117nhp at 200psi; the engine was built by Swan Hunter & Wigham Richardson of Newcastle.

In 1946 *Sea Alarm* was formally acquired by the Clyde Shipping Company, and her name was changed to *Flying Fulmar*. She continued to work in the Clyde until 1956, when she was sold to the Alarm Steam Tug Company Ltd, of Bristol, a company owned by C. J. King & Sons Ltd. She then worked in the Bristol Channel, coaling regularly at Barry, until 1973, when she was withdrawn from service and sold in 1977 to the Welsh Industrial & Maritime Museum at Cardiff. She was duly placed in West Dock Basin and the remainder was filled in, leaving her land-locked. As part of a job creation project she was placed on a concrete base so that she was preserved in a dry condition; in a second job creation project the tug was restored both internally and externally, and for many years was visited by educational groups. However, despite great protest this lovely old vessel was cut up for scrap in July 1998, and at the same time the nearby Welsh Industrial & Maritime Museum was closed, a fatality of the Cardiff Bay redevelopment programme.

Impressive in the background of this view is the Cardiff Railway Company's headquarters, the Pierhead Building, and to its right are the Channel Dry Docks. *Associated British Ports*

Below A survivor of the redevelopment was the former Customs & Excise House, photographed on 29 April 1987, when it was being used by the Trentham Company Ltd. This Grade II listed building was jacked up and moved in its entirety, inch by inch, to its new site 100 yards away, displaced by plans for a new road to take traffic into the Cardiff Bay development area. Today it has been converted for use as a restaurant. *Author*

Bute West Dock

Moving northwards up the west side of Bute West Dock, first were the warehouses and moorings of the South Wales & Liverpool Steam Packet company; one of these would later become 'V' Warehouse, of corrugated-iron construction with one floor, measuring 191 feet long by 46 feet wide, and used for the storage of general goods. Also alongside this wharf were the buildings of the London Steam Packet Company, which by 1901 were to become 'C' and 'T' Warehouses. 'C' Warehouse was a wooden building with one floor, 323 feet long by 50 feet wide, and held general goods, while 'T' Warehouse was of corrugated iron with one floor, measuring 80 feet by 50 feet, also accommodating general goods

Next came a combination of various warehouses and buildings, which, on the map of 1913, consisted of a grain warehouse and others for various purposes, as well as a wire rope works. This was the West Bute Wire Rope Works owned by Messrs George Elliot & Company Ltd, which opened in 1894. Here also the firm of Messrs Morgan & Sanders had set up its rope-making factory by 1855. Then followed a mill and some more warehouses. Somewhere along this west side of West Dock was 'I' shed, which was of corrugated-iron construction, measured 180 feet long by 50 feet wide, and was used for the storage of general goods.

Finally, in the top north-west corner was a flour mill and a Public Wharf. The mill was located alongside a canal feeder, the West Junction Canal, which joined with the Glamorganshire Canal after passing under the TVR lines going to Queen Street Station and under Bute Street (the first dry dock was built not far from here, on the East Canal Wharf in 1829). The feeder then passed between the timber yards of Messrs John Bland & Co on one side and Messrs Watson's on the other. It is of note that this flour mill was established by Joel Spiller and Samuel Browne, corn and flour merchants, in 1854; later, in 1890, the firm became a partnership of Messrs Spillers & Company Ltd and William Baker & Sons (of Bristol), to form the firm of Spillers & Baker Ltd, flour millers. By 1913 the firm was sending its products all over the world from this dock.

A short distance behind the mill and also behind the waterfront buildings ran Collingdon Road. Retracing our steps southwards along this

'Embarkation of the remains of the lamented, the most noble, John Crichton Stuart, Marquis of Bute, at Bute West Dock, on 30 March 1848.' *Associated British Ports*

road, we pass the backs of the quayside buildings on the west side. Sandwiched between this road and the TVR lines was a collection of timber yards. Messrs Watson's was the biggest, with a somewhat smaller yard belonging to Messrs Hestell & Co; each had its respective sawmills. The Midland Wagon Works, seen on the 1882 map, had disappeared by 1901, the area becoming part of Watson's timber yard, with its sawmill located behind the warehouses of the South Wales & Liverpool Steam Packet company. Seen on the 1913 map, this yard had become even bigger.

As seen on the 1920 map, located behind the grain warehouse and Collingdon Road was the Bute Dock Foundry, and a little further northwards were the premises of the Glyn Mill Corn Co, between the mill and the wire rope works. Also by this time some of the warehouses had been converted into a flour mill with a granary alongside; situated north of the wire and rope works was Castle Mill, for the milling of corn.

Returning to the top of West Dock, there was another Public Wharf, and situated next to it a second dock feeder canal, which went into yet another Junction Canal, only this time continuing northwards, passing under Herbert Street, to reach the premises and timber yards of Messrs Robinson, David & Co Ltd, before passing between Pembroke Terrace and Edward Terrace. Later both canal and terraces would become the present-day Churchill Way. Next to this feeder was a dry dock, constructed in 1849 by Messrs Charles Hill & Sons of Bristol and measuring 235 feet long by 38 feet wide; on the map of 1920 this has become a graving dock, the Bute West Graving Dock. (In 1957 the measurements are given as 235 feet by 40 feet.) The northern end of this graving dock was next to Herbert Street, with a pedestrian walkway alongside the entrance gate into West Dock. The 1920 map also shows that each of the nearby Public Wharfs had one crane, and there were also two cranes at the South Wales & Liverpool Steam Packet wharf, midway up the west side of the dock.

The previously mentioned West Junction Canal, which ran between West Dock and the Glamorganshire Canal, also provided access to two timber ponds, covering an area of 28 acres with a depth of between 8 and 10 feet; one was close to West Canal Wharf and the other close to the River Taff at the point where the Penarth

Road bridge spanned the river. The feeder canal provided a ready supply of water to these ponds, en route to the West Dock.

Returning to the bottom of Bute West Dock and travelling up the east side, the first feature, first seen on the 1901 map, was the Junction Dry Dock, alongside which was an engineering works; the 1920 map shows a travelling crane on the east side of the dry dock. Beside the works was the wooden Scandinavian or Norwegian Chapel. The east side of West Dock was for the shipping of coal, and the 1882 map shows the location of the coaling staiths, each with its respective weighing machine alongside. On the 1913 map the mooring posts are marked as mooring rings.

The feeding of coal into ships' holds was a constant process, fed by an almost limitless number of the many and varied private colliery wagons that were mainly brought to the dock over the metals of the Taff Vale Railway network, via its East Branch.

Heading further north past the staiths we come to some travelling cranes, then a corn mill, near which is a fixed crane. Beyond was another canal feeder, this one also going into a Junction Canal between the West and East Docks. At the West Dock entrance of this feeder are eight mooring posts. Finally we reach the previously mentioned graving dock at the top of the dock.

By the Second World War the former coaling staiths were marked on maps as coaling hoists, and their numbers were much reduced; only six remained in 1941, and only four were in use by 1946, renumbered from the middle of the dock southwards Nos 1, 2, 3 and 4. Between 1 and 2, and 2 and 3, a 1946 map clearly shows that two of these coaling tips, as they have again been renamed, are being taken out of commission. The decline of the coal industry had began. By this time also there are mooring rings rather than posts, and the large reservoir, close to the iron foundry and the Junction Dry Dock, has gone.

On 31 January 1964 Bute West Dock was closed to trade, and in 1970 was filled in. However, it was not until 1985, some 15 years later, that the remaining buildings that had served this original dock for many years were finally demolished and the ground levelled. By the end of 1987 the last remnants of this historic dock were gone, and the area was ready for the Cardiff Bay Development

Group to begin its reshaping. By 1990 only Collingdon Road, on the west side, provided any idea of the grandness of the redevelopment that was occurring in this docklands area, with Herbert Street and nearby Tyndall Street providing the northern boundary to the development area.

The docks were governed by a set of bye-laws and regulations, such as these from the period 1886/87:

Bute Docks Cardiff
William Thomas Lewis, General Manager
20th July 1886

All vessels entering or within these docks are under the control of the dock master. Any person who refuses or neglects to comply will be liable to a penalty.

A stemming book is kept by the dock master into which masters of vessels are required to enter the name and tonnage of their vessel, nature of cargo, draught of water drawn, and names of brokers, if any. Untrue entries: penalty imposed £5.

Preferences may be given to steamers over sailing vessels, or to vessels with cargoes over those with ballast. Vessels must not remain or be left in these docks, basins, or entrance channel, without their master on board, or without permission of the dock master: penalty imposed £5.

If a master of a vessel in these docks refuses to proceed to sea against the judgement of the dock master, then he may lose her turn and be removed to a place in these docks as directed: penalty imposed £5.

No vessel may berth or move from her berth without permission: penalty imposed £5.

No vessel may navigates by steam in the docks without permission: penalty £5.

Any vessel in these docks will have the master aboard, or he will have appointed a proper and competent person to take charge in his absence, otherwise penalty imposed £5.

The sails of any vessel in the docks will be stowed or kept furled, and will not be loosened without permission: penalty imposed £5.

Any person who makes fast any rope or chain to a shed, lamp post, coal staith, or anything not assigned for the purpose: penalty imposed £5.

Any person who casts off, cuts, breaks or destroys the mooring or fastening of any vessel not his own: penalty imposed £5.

Any master who causes a vessel to be careened, heaved down, smoked, greaved or breamed [various means of cleaning] without permission: penalty imposed £5.

The hatchways of every vessel laden or being laden with coal must be left open and not closed until beyond the limits of the dock master's authority: penalty imposed £2. Any vessel found with closed hatches: penalty imposed £2.

All dust, ashes, and other refuse deposited must be with permission: penalty imposed £2. No vessel is to be washed, swept and cleaned while in these docks: penalty imposed £2. All dogs aboard these vessels must be tied up: penalty imposed £2.

As to vessels in Dock:

All vessels on entering the Bute Docks must have their boom irons taken off, their yards braced, sharpen up on the port braces, and kept in that position during their stay in dock, jib and flying jib booms rigged into the cap, with anchor stock awash, and clear for letting go. When vessels are lying in the tiers their anchors must be let go, and kept down during stormy weather, and they must have mooring ropes to the shore on the windward side, especially when the storm cone is hoisted. Liability for damage will rest with the master of the vessel not complying with the above conditions.

Above This Ernest T. Bush postcard shows Cardiff Docks in about 1900. A single-track railway line crosses over the Inner Lock by a swing bridge, and beyond is Bute West Dock, with the buildings of the Junction Dry Dock over to the right, while over on the far left can be seen the lines and buildings of the Taff Vale Railway. *G. G. Jones*

Right The swingbridge, which provided pedestrian and railway access over the Inner Lock, is seen again here in about 1910. Operated by hydraulic machinery, it opened when needed, allowing vessels to pass through. *Associated British Ports*

Below Snippets of maritime news from the *Pontypridd Chronicle*, 20 March 1885. *Pontypridd Library*

The Liverpool steamer Alleghany, which left Cardiff on the 9th January, is reported to have been lost in the heavy gales of the two days following her departure. It is feared that the crew, twenty-nine in number, have all perished.

The steamer Cambria of Cardiff, and the barque Chinampas, of Pictou, collided near Cardiff. The steamer anchored in the Roads for repairs, and the barque docked at Penarth with the loss of jibboom.

The screw steamer Longueil, Captain Read, belonging to Messrs Morel Bros., Cardiff, left Cardiff on Saturday for Hull, to load a cargo of railway material and carriages for the Suakim-Berber Railway.

Left Captured German U-boat No 1023 on show to the public on 17 June 1945, moored in Bute West Dock. The warehouses on the left are the plywood storage warehouses of Messrs Robinson, David & Co Ltd. *Associated British Ports*

Below left A shipment label to Robinson, David & Co Ltd by the SS *Nora*. *A. G. Powell collection*

Below The Missionary Society's new vessel, the *John Williams VI*, is at anchorage in Bute West Dock in August 1948 prior to taking up missionary duties in the Fiji Islands. The photograph gives us another view of the brick-built, corrugated-roofed warehouses of Messrs Robinson, David & Co, whose head office was in Herbert Street, Cardiff. The warehouses were also known as 'V', 'C', and 'T' Sheds. Also in view are the coaling staiths of West Dock, and the high-level lines over on the east side. Behind the vessel on the right is the Scandinavian Chapel, while in the foreground are a varied assortment of single-deck coaches; the two on the extreme left are unidentified, but the remainder, from left to right, are an AEC, as Bedford WTB (on the road), an AEC Regal, and lastly a Bedford OB. *Associated British Ports*

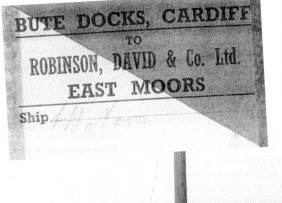

BUTE DOCKS, CARDIFF
TO
ROBINSON, DAVID & Co. Ltd.
EAST MOORS

Ship

Right The wooden Scandinavian Chapel is seen again in this view of the 'Triumphal Arch' erected over the main gateway into Cardiff Docks from James Street. It was constructed by the Civil Engineering Department as part of the Coronation decorations of June 1953. *Associated British Ports*

Above Cardiff Railway engine No 14, an 0-6-0ST built by Messrs Parfitt & Jenkins in 1872, crosses Bute Street, at the junction of James Street, to pass through the dock gates in 1905. It is hauling a solitary seven-plank wagon of coal from the Universal Colliery. No 14 was withdrawn from service in 1916. *Cardiff Central Library, Local Studies Department*

Below This wooden masted vessel is at anchor in Bute West Dock; it is very difficult to identify the location, but it could be the north west (or top) side, with the footbridge spanning the dock feeder that passed under Herbert Street en route to the timber yards of Messrs Robinson, David & Co. The ship is moored alongside the Public Wharf, and looks to be undergoing general repairs to her hull; there are freshly sawn wooden planks, step-ladders, and plenty of activity going on alongside. The carved maiden at the bow, under the bowsprit, adds a touch of elegance to this old lady of the seas, photographed in about 1880. *Associated British Ports*

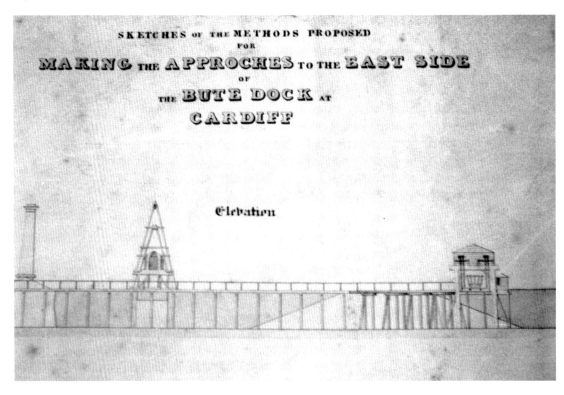

SKETCHES of the METHODS PROPOSED
FOR
MAKING the APPROCHES to the EAST SIDE
OF
THE BUTE DOCK AT
CARDIFF

Elevation

Above A sketch by Robert Stephenson 'of the methods proposed for making the approaches to the east side of the Bute Dock', dated 8 February 1847. Stephenson was involved with the development of the Bute Docks as engineer and architect, including the entrance to the Bute Dock Ship Canal in 1840, the Bute Dock Basin and Bute West Dock, with its wharfs and the land development around it. While thus employed Stephenson had thoughts for a new type of coal tip, whereby a fully loaded coal wagon would be held in place above the vessel, then tilted to allow the coal to slide down into the ship's hold. From 1851 to the opening of Bute East Dock Stephenson acted as arbitrator to settle any differences or problems that arose. *Associated British Ports*

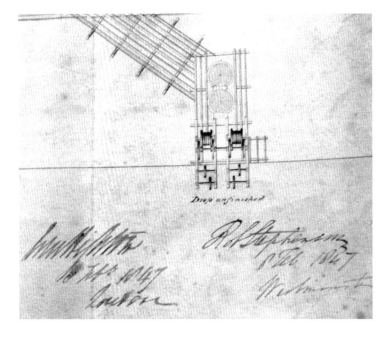

Drop unfinished

Left Another sketch, bearing the same date, shows an unfinished coal drop. *Associated British Ports*

Further sketches showing the arrangements for the operation of
Stephenson's proposed coal drops, circa 1847. *Associated British Ports*

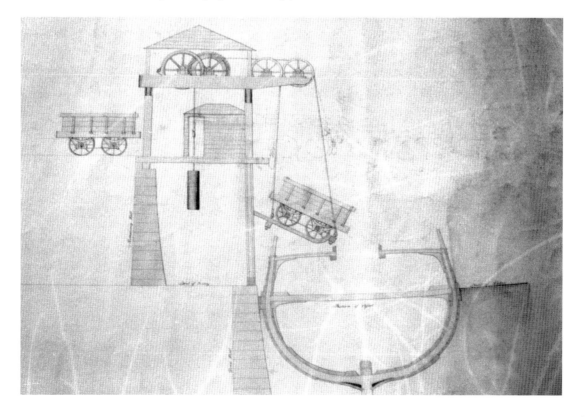

Opposite page Photographed from the deck of a vessel at 3.45pm on 25 April 1884, two very different types of coaling tips are seen here on the east side of West Dock. The round-topped type, on the extreme left, is in the process of coaling up what looks like a small coaster, while in the centre is No 12 tip. Behind the tips can be seen the masts of ships moored in Bute East Dock.

The second view of No 12 tip was taken at 3.40pm on 29 April 1884; in the bottom left-hand corner, standing alongside a vessel registered in Sarpsborg, Norway, is a young man, possibly a guide or assistant to the unknown photographer. *Associated British Ports*

Below This magnificent shot is a close-up of high-level tip No 10, of a type also known as balance tips. On the right-hand side is what appears to be a wheel, perhaps part of the hydraulic action that moved the rams slowly forward to push the hold of the vessel into position under the coaling chute, or, more importantly, to stop the vessel from touching and damaging the coaling tip. On the left-hand side is a loaded bucket, which is probably the counter balance needed for the chute to retain its upright position. These tips were stoutly made of thick wooden timbers, and built to last.

The photograph was taken in the West Dock at 11.00am on 28 April 1884. It will have been made with a half-size glass negative, placed individually into the back of the camera, with a hood placed over both camera and cameraman to prevent light from spoiling the picture. The view would then be focused in, appearing upside-down. The whole contraption was placed on a tripod for steadiness, and the time taken for exposure was estimated by skill and experience alone, judging from the time of day and amount of light needed, not to mention the conditions around where it was taken – from the deck of a vessel in the dock, probably a fairly large rowing-boat, that would certainly be moving about. All this was happening while our unknown photographer focused in on his carefully selected subject. Then, once exposed, the glass negative would be placed in a sealed container, all of these procedures being carried out while still under the protective darkness of the hood, until the negative could be developed at a later stage, using chemicals that, if used too long, would gradually poison the human body and cause blindness or even death. It therefore seems a minor miracle that these photographs came out, or were taken, at all! *Associated British Ports*

Below An extract from the GWR ports magazine, circa 1927. *Associated British Ports*

MEASUREMENTS OF COAL AND COKE.

The following is an indication of what space is required for one ton of the following combustibles. It must only be taken as an indication, because considerable differences are noted from time to time in the stowage capacity of shipments of the same coal in the same vessel. The figures given are those at time of shipment :—

1.	Cardiff Best Large, about	42·5 to 43 cubic feet to the ton.	
2.	Cardiff Bituminous Large	42·5 to 45	,, ,,
3.	Newport Large	42·5 to 45	,, ,,
4.	Cardiff Through	41·5 to 42·5	,, ,,
5.	Cardiff Small	44	,, ,,
6.	Beehive Foundry Coke	84	,, ,,
7.	Modern Coke Oven Coke	78 to 80	,, ,,
8.	Gas Coke	80	,, ,,
9.	Patent Fuel	35 to 37	,, ,,
10.	Anthracite Large	40 to 42	,, ,,
11.	Anthracite Cobbles	45 to 47	,, ,,
12.	North Country Large	46 to 47	,, ,,

Differences in Prices of Coals at various Bristol Channel Ports.

Owing to geographical conditions, and the situation of Railways serving certain districts, prices of most coals vary considerably at South Wales and other Bristol Channel ports.

Generally speaking, the ports of Cardiff, Barry and Penarth, are equally served in this respect, and except for a group of coals to the westward of the Cardiff district, the prices of coals at these three ports are the same. At Newport, the situation is different. For shipment at that port, the so-called Cardiff coals cost somewhat more, generally about 2d. to 3d. per ton above their prices f.o.b. at Cardiff, while coals from the Monmouthshire Valleys generally cost 6d. per ton more for shipment at Cardiff, Barry and Penarth than at Newport. In some cases, coals can only be brought with great difficulty from certain collieries for shipment outside certain docks, on account of agreements between Colliery owners and these docks, or on account of coal landlords' stipulations for traffic to be sent to certain dock or docks. It can be roughly estimated that Cardiff semi-bituminous large coals can be bought at the same prices f.o.b. at Cardiff, Penarth and Barry, 2d. to 3d. extra at Newport, 6d. to 1/6 extra at Swansea, and 3d. to 1/- extra at Port Talbot. Cardiff Dry Steam Coals can generally be bought at the same prices f.o.b. at Cardiff, Penarth, Barry, and Port Talbot, 3d. extra at Newport. Certain coals in the Western Cardiff district can be shipped at Port Talbot at the same price as at Cardiff.

COMING to the particularising theme. we find that BEST CARDIFF ADMIRALTYS are moderately firm at about 12s. 9d.—while the whole of 13s. is softly breathed as a quotation, in certain instances. Mind you, it is only a breathed affair as yet. for we can find no record of the figures having been reached, in actual business. In the latter instance, as you might readily guess, the quotation emanates from the coalowner who is the fortunate possessor of a full stem (and a fuller gall), and has, therefore, little to spare, just now! Furthermore, there are quite a few collieries in this grade, whose engagements are sufficient to comfortably tide them over the present month. In their case, additional stemming is naturally difficult, and the quotation is given with rather more than a pretence of firmness. All the same, the actual value of BESTS pans out to 12s. 9d. as an average—which means that quite a few are willing to discuss the relative beauties which coruscate around a possible 12s. 6d., "If you'll make it large and prompt," yes.

SECONDS are showing some little attempt at steadiness, although the demand has been insufficient, so far. to enable sellers to raise prices—which continue at about last levels, if the conditions of the particular colliery involved is allowed for. With regard to figures —quoted figures, you understand—these range around from 12s. to 12s. 6d., and the top qualities are being really maintained at the latter, as stems are good enough to admit of this. But for the average SECOND, the former figures are about the actual value. There is no great activity here, but as already stated, steadiness is in evidence, although the demand is somewhat limited.

ORDINARIES continue in a state of easiness: values likewise: these latter, being expressed in figures, will be written as ranging from 11s. 6d. to 12s.—according to the variety implicated. There is but little new business coming forward, and while prices are unaltered (for the reason that nothing has transpired to warrant any alteration) there is but little doubt that anything of a tempting nature, would work a reduction in short order. Nice state of affairs, isn't it? To see that prices continue "as they were," merely because nobody seems to be in any undue hurry to buy the stuff! But the figures quoted have been obtained in one or two instances, although buyers are too few to stimulate, or otherwise, this section of the coal trade.

DRYS may not be said to have assimilated any additional steadiness, for their old-time inactivity—that masterly condition which has been theirs of late—continues. Naturally, this same condition keeps the grade in a weak state, and promptly, good coals could be obtained at 11s. 6d. Indeed, for anything required for this position, BESTS are readily obtainable at 11s. 9d. stems, all 'round, being dishearteningly easy, with supplies greatly in excess of the demand.

MONMOUTHSHIRE COAL. There is but little that is new to report in connection with this phase of local industry. For immediate requirements, prices have ruled as firmly as last week —more particularly in the case of BLACK VEINS, and stems for which are, at the moment, somewhat tight. Moreover, Collieries here are well supplied with a good show of tonnage. For prices, we find them mainly as at our last time of writing—11s. 9d., which figure it is difficult to improve upon.

ORDINARIES, too, are in fairly good demand, for the quotation is steady at 11s. 6d. All the same, there is no undue amount of business passing herein, at least, above 11s. 3d., and ORDINARIES may not be truthfully written as worth anything above this, at the moment. Even the so-called sympathy with the premier sorts has had no visible effect, in this direction, for restriction of output is the one condition which is operative in this particular grade.

SECONDS have hardened. This, consequent upon an improved demand, which has resulted in a filling of stems. The sellers' idea is around from 10s. 3d. to 10s. 6d., and as in other quarters, the bulk of the transactions have been for prompt loading, forward business being altogether slow and disappointing.

RHONDDA No. 3's are an unchanged section. Values show a maintenance of those ruling at our last—13s. 6d. to 13s. 9d.; but they are easy inclined, rather than otherwise. Stems are fairly good, and this, of course, keeps collieries well-employed; but outside of these engagements, business is the reverse of brisk.

RHONDDA No. 2's, having experienced a good week in the matter of demand, are firmer. Supplies, on this account, have been somewhat restricted, and the quantity available at an early date, being anything but considerable, prices have ruled in the close neighbourhood of 10s. which has been paid, too.

SMALL COALS. Here, once again, you have the redeeming feature of the market. The demand continues great as ever; the supply equally restricted—the latter accounted for by fulness of stems, and approaching holidays. BESTS have readily commanded 9s., and at the time of writing. 9s. 6d. is the quotation—although this is scarcely applicable, seeing that dealers have none to sell! SECONDS have ranged between 8s. 6d. and 9s., while for ORDINARIES, there has been a flattering demand at 8s. 6d. Other vagaries, we give below, although NEWPORTS have advanced considerably during the last day or so, present value for BESTS of that ilk, being around by 8s. 6d.

PATENT FUELS are steady—not so much on positive business, as because of the firmness of SMALLS. Average values are at 13s. 3d. PITWOOD, which is quoted at from 19s. 6d. to 19s. 9d., is much firmer than of late.

APPROXIMATE FIGURES FOR THE WEEK, ARE AS FOLLOW:— CARDIFF. August 2. 1905.

(All quotations f.o.b. at the respective ports of shipment.)

QUALITY.	THURSDAY.	FRIDAY.	SATURDAY.	MONDAY.	TUESDAY.	WEDNESDAY.
Best Cardiff Ad'alty Large	12s. 7½d.	12s. 6d., 12s. 9d.	12s. 9d.	12s. 6d., 13s. 0d.	12s. 9d.	12s. 9d., 13s. 0d.
Second Ditto. ,, ...	11s. 9d., 12s. 3d.	12s. 0d.	12s. 0d.	12s. 0d., 12s. 3d.	12s. 1½d.	12s. 3d.
Other Second Cardiff ,, ...	11s. 6d., 12s. 0d.	11s. 6d.	11s. 6d.	11s. 9d.	11s. 6d., 12s. 0d.	11s. 0d.
Drys ,, ...	11s. 7½d.	11s. 6d.	11s. 6d., 11s. 9d.	11s. 9d.	11s. 6d., 12s. 0d.	11s. 9d.
Best Newport ,, ...	11s. 6d., 12s. 0d.	11s. 6d.	11s. 6d., 12s. 0d.	12s. 0d.	11s. 9d.	11s. 9d., 12s. 0d.
Ordinary Bests ,, ...	11s. 3d.	11s. 3d., 11s. 6d.	11s. 4½d.	11s. 4½d.	11s. 6d.	11s. 6d.
Seconds ,, ...	10s. 3d.	10s. 3d., 10s. 6d.	10s. 4½d.	10s. 6d.	10s. 3d., 10s. 6d.	10s. 6d.
Best House Coal ,, ...	14s. 6d., 11s. 9d.	14s. 7½d.	14s. 6d.	14s. 6d.	14s. 0d., 14s. 6d.	14s. 3d.
No. 3 Rhondda ,, ...	13s. 6d.	13s. 9d.	13s. 7½d.	13s. 7½d.	13s. 6d.	13s. 6d.
No. 2 Ditto. ,, ...	9s. 9d.	9s. 10½d.	9s. 9d., 10s. 0d.	10s. 0d.	10s. 0d.	9s. 9d., 10s. 3d.
Rhondda 3 " Thro." ...	11s. 9d.	11s. 9d.	11s. 7½d.	11s. 6d., 11s. 9d.	11s. 9d.	11s. 6d.
,, 2 ,, ...	8s. 6d.	8s. 6d.	8s. 6d.	8s. 6d.	8s. 6d., 9s. 0d.	8s. 6d.
Smalls:—						
Best Cardiff ...	8s. 9d., 9s. 0d.	8s. 10½d.	9s. 0d.	9s. 0d.	9s. 0d., 9s. 3d.	9s. 0d., 9s. 3d.
Seconds ...	8s. 6d.	8s. 7½d.	8s. 9d.	8s. 10½d.	8s. 9d., 9s. 0d.	8s. 6d.
Ordinaries ...	8s. 3d.	8s. 3d., 8s. 6d.	8s. 4½d.	8s. 6d.	8s. 6d.	8s. 3d., 8s. 6d.
Best Newport ...	7s. 9d.	7s. 9d.	8s. 0d.	8s. 0d.	8s. 0d.	8s. 0d.
Seconds ...	7s. 6d.	7s. 6d.	7s. 9d.	7s. 9d.	7s. 6d., 7s. 9d.	8s. 0d.
Rhondda No. 2 ...	7s. 6d., 7s. 9d.	7s. 9d.	7s. 9d.	8s. 0d.	8s. 0d., 8s. 6d.	8s. 0d.
,, No. 3 ...	9s. 6d., 10s. 0d.	9s. 9d.	9s. 9d.	9s. 7½d.	9s. 6d.	9s. 6d.
Foundry Coke:—						
Special ...	21s. 3d.	21s. 3d.	21s. 0d., 21s. 6d.	21s. 3d., 21s. 6d.	21s. 6d.	21s. 3d.
Ordinary ...	17s. 9d.	17s. 9d.	17s. 6d.	17s. 6d.	17s. 6d., 17s. 9d.	17s. 9d.
Furnace Coke ...	16s. 3d.	16s. 6d.	16s. 6d.	16s. 0d., 16s. 6d.	16s. 3d.	16s. 0d., 16s. 3d.
Patent Fuel ...	13s. 0d.	13s. 0d.	12s. 9d., 13s. 3d.	13s. 3d.	13s. 0d., 13s. 6d.	13s. 6d.
Pitwood (ex ship) .	19s. 6d.	19s. 6d.	19s. 9d.	19s. 0d.	19s. 6d., 19s. 9d.	19s. 7½d.

All, less 2½ per cent. discount, with payment at thirty days. except where otherwise stated.
All quotations for large Coals imply Colliery Screened.

THE MARITIME REVIEW.

The Coal and Shipping Exchange, in Mount Stuart Square, was known locally simply as the Exchange, and here is an insight into coal prices and a way of life now gone from Cardiff, from *The Maritime Review* dated 4 August 1905.

Right Pitwood stacked up and ready at Cardiff Docks, probably on the east side of Bute West Dock. In the foreground men are using double-handed wood saws, while a Lewis Hunter 3-ton luffing crane (one with its jib hinged at its lower ends) can be seen behind, circa 1905. *Associated British Ports*

Right More pitwood – this photograph, again, circa 1905, clearly shows the volume of timber that entered the docks on an almost daily business. These stacking grounds covered a vast area, and must have held numerous dangers for the men working there. *Associated British Ports*

Below A pair of redundant ferries, *Severn Queen* and *Severn King*, previously used for the transportation of passengers and cars across the River Severn but displaced by the opening of the first Severn Bridge, are laid up in West Dock in about 1965. G. *Morgan*

Top Messrs Neale & West's new oil-burning trawler *Akita*, CF.4, is berthed at the Fish Quay on the east side of West Dock on 18 June 1939. The water in the dock can be seen to be at sill level, and in the left background the Scandinavian Chapel is seen again. *Associated British Ports*

Above The scene on 6 March 1987, taken from almost the same place as the previous photograph some 48 years earlier, shows that the West Dock has long been filled in, and now it is time for the remaining buildings to be bulldozed, although the Scandinavian Chapel would be saved and moved to a new site. Behind it can be seen modern cranes erecting buildings as part of the new Cardiff Bay development. To the right of the chapel are the remains of the Falkland Island Company's premises, behind which is the Ice Factory (the name of the long building with the rounded gable end is unknown), while in front of the buildings, now filled in, is the site of the former Junction Dry Dock. *Author*

Left Seen on the same day, and also awaiting demolition, are the premises of C. R. Kerman & Sons Ltd (Engineers Merchants), who sold engineering sundries, spanners, nuts bolts, etc. Located behind this building were the offices of the Junction Dry Dock Co, and in the background is the Scandinavian Chapel. *Author*

2. BUTE EAST DOCK

Construction on the first part of Bute East Dock started in January 1852 and it was opened on 20 July 1855. It was 1,000 feet long and 300 feet long. Once this first part had been completed, the engineers, Messrs Walker, Burgess and Cooper, started work on the first part of the extension, which was completed and opened in 1857; the length of the dock was now 2,000 feet and its width 500 feet. The final extension was officially started in January 1858, being 2,300 feet long with a width also of 500 feet. On 14 September 1859 the East Dock was finally opened to trade, and, as previously mentioned, was also leased to the TVR, which initially used the coal tips located on the west side, served by sidings with a total capacity of 872 wagons. Bute East Dock closed in 1970.

On Saturday 30 January 1858 the *Cardiff & Merthyr Guardian* reported to its readers on the opening of the Bute East Dock Extension:

'In our impressions of last week, we briefly alluded to this event; we are now enabled to give additional particulars, chiefly as to the prospective advantages likely to result to the trade of the port of Cardiff.

On Tuesday the 19th inst, Mr Boyle, the acting trustee of the Marquis of Bute, accompanied by Lieutenant Dornford, the dock master; Mr Clark, mining engineer; Mr McConnochie, the resident dock engineer (acting for Messrs Walter, Burgess and Cooper); Messrs Hemingway's and Pearson, the dock contractors; and Mr Smithson and Mr Page, the chief officials of the Rhymney Railway, made a formal opening of this important sheet of water, by towing the beautiful barque the *Cornelia of Leith*, about 700 tons register, from that portion of the East Dock which has been in use about two and a half years into the extension dock.

Our readers will be interested to learn that this extension is in extent 20 acres, with a depth of water of 25 feet and a width of 500 feet. This auxiliary dock accommodation

The opening of Bute East Dock as it appeared in **The Illustrated London News** of **1 October 1859.** *Courtesy of The Illustrated London News Picture Library*

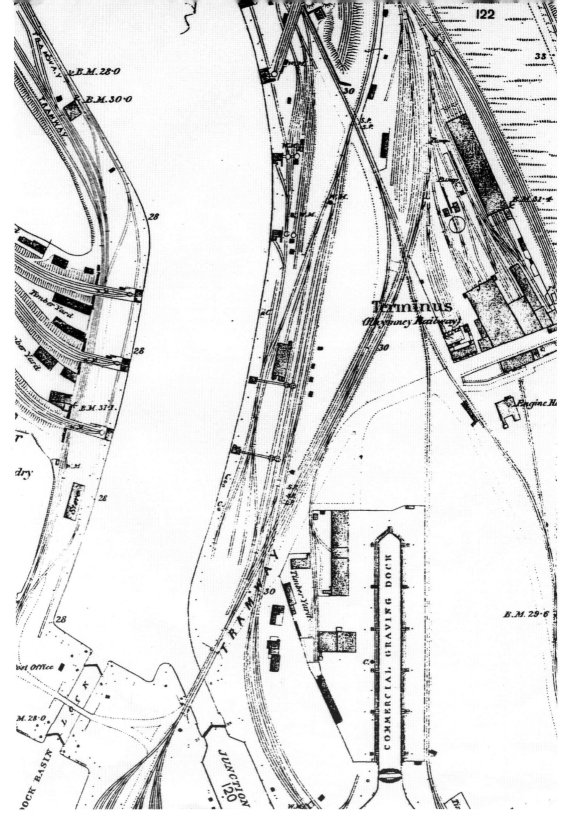

Ordnance Survey map of 1882, showing the Rhymney Railway terminus on the right, with its turntable and engine sheds, and part of Bute East Dock, showing Junction Lock (bottom) and Commercial Dry Dock. *Crown copyright*

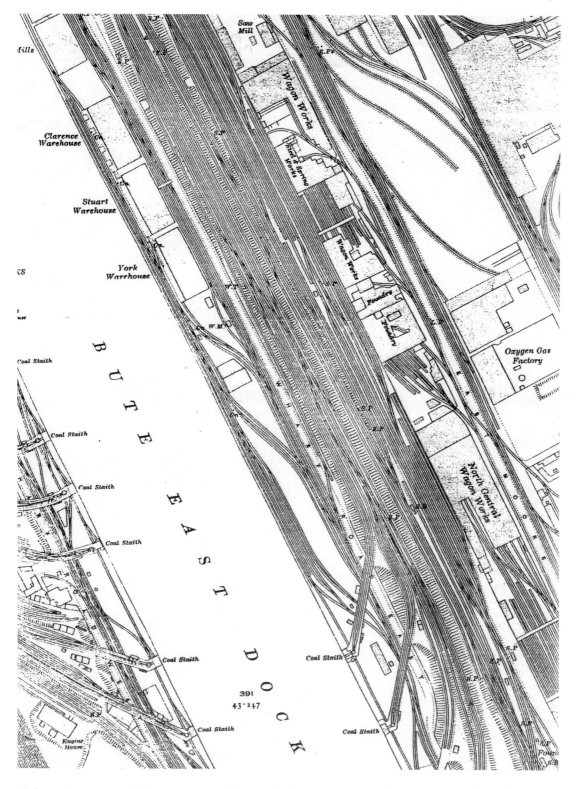

Ordnance Survey map of 1920, showing part of Bute East Dock and the position of Clarence, Stuart and York Warehouses, as well as the various wagon works that occupied the area to the right of the busy coaling lines. *Crown copyright*

20° & 21° VICTORIÆ, *Cap.*cxl.

Rhymney Railway Act, 1857.

SCHEDULE to which the foregoing Act refers.

MEMORANDUM OF AGREEMENT dated this Thirty-first Day of March One thousand eight hundred and fifty-one.

It is agreed between the South Wales Railway Company of the First Part, and the Right Honourable Lord James Stuart, Onesiphorus Tyndall Bruce, and James Munro Macnabb, as Representatives of the late Marquis of Bute, of the Second Part, as follows:

First. The South Wales Railway Company shall abandon the Branch Railways proposed in their Bill now before Parliament to the Glamorganshire Canal and the Bute Dock.

Second. In consideration of such Abandonment, the Parties hereto of the Second Part undertake to expend a Sum of Money not exceeding One hundred and eighty thousand Pounds in the Execution of Works for a new Dock or Basin at Cardiff to the East of the existing Docks, with a new Entrance to the present Cut (unless Mr. Robert Stephenson shall be of opinion that such new Entrance is unnecessary), with all proper and usual Quays, Landing Places, and other Works and Conveniences connected therewith, such Dock to be constructed of a greater Depth than the present Dock, according to a Plan to be agreed upon between the Parties, and in case of Difference between them according to a Plan to be prepared by Mr. Robert Stephenson as Arbitrator acting indifferently between the Parties.

Third. That such Dock and other Works shall be proceeded with with all reasonable Despatch, and so at least to permit of its being opened and Accommodation afforded for shipping Goods and Minerals therein on or before the First Day of September One thousand eight hundred and fifty-three.

Fourth. The South Wales Railway Company to apply if necessary to Parliament in the next Session for Power to construct a Branch Railway to and along the East Side of the said proposed Dock, according to a Plan and Section to be determined on by the Engineer of that Company, and to construct such Branch Railway so as that it shall be opened on or before the First September One thousand eight hundred and fifty-three; and the Parties hereto of the Second Part, in consideration of the Trade which will be brought to the said Dock by means of such Branch, to grant a Lease for Two hundred and fifty Years of the Land necessary for the Construction of such Branch, the Rent to be estimated upon a fair and reasonable Valuation of the present Value of the Land, without reference to the proposed new Dock, and to be converted into a Tonnage Rate upon the Articles conveyed thereon, such Rent to be so ascertained and determined by Mr. Robert Stephenson.

Left The Schedule of the Rhymney Railway Act of 1857, giving authority to Robert Stephenson to act as arbitrator between the parties and to oversee the work taking place on the new Bute East Dock, and to ascertain and decide on the rents and tolls to be paid at his discretion. Stephenson was born in 1803 and had been responsible for the construction and completion of the Conway Bridges in 1848, the Montreal Bridge and High Level Bridge, Newcastle upon Tyne, in 1849, and the Royal Border Bridge, Berwick upon Tweed, and Britannia Tubular Bridge in 1850; he was a Member of Parliament for 12 years, but sadly he died in 1859. *Author's collection*

Below From the *Barry Dock Tide Table and Year Book,* 1891. *L. D. Bryant collection*

must be regarded as of great importance for the port of Cardiff, and will not fail to aid materially the development of the mineral resources of the Eastern and most valuable portion of the South Wales mineral basin, by its affording the means of shipment of a large quantity of produce.

The dock purse does not, of course, meet all the requirements of a heavy mineral and iron traffic; a great deal more is required. Considerable works have been, and are being made for giving adequate facilities for the shipment of goods. At the present time there are three coal staiths on the Western side of East Dock, approached from the Taff Vale Railway, and on the Eastern side there are four staiths belonging to the Rhymney Railway Company; the latter are nearly ready to be used. In addition the trustees are erecting five staiths on the Western side, making a total of 12 staiths on the East Dock. Of this number, three are in working order, four will be ready in a very short time, and the remaining five in about three months, the whole representing a coal traffic of one million tons, to which may be added the Rhymney Iron Company's traffic of say 100,000 tons, and taking the traffic from other sources at 100,000 tons, we have an aggregate traffic for the East Dock of 1,200,000 tons. If we take the exports and imports of Cardiff in the year 1857, in round numbers, at 2,000,000 tons, we can properly estimate the extent of this additional dock accommodation, which as the figures indicate exceeds one half of the present trade of the port. Be it understood that this is not the maximum trade which may be done; a large quay of water frontage remains unoccupied, on which six staiths may be conveniently erected, which six staiths would afford a proportionate rate of shipment.

Moreover, the trustees believing in the generally received opinion of the valuable resources of the district through which the Taff Vale and other railways, having their termini at Cardiff, traverse, have not hesitated to afford a further extension of the Bute Dock, which is now in progress, and which will most probably be completed this year, this further extension will be 15 acres, making the float or dock, exclusive of the basin or locks, 42 acres, the whole representing, when completed, shipping accommodation equal to the entire trade of Cardiff, at the present time, and forming, perhaps, the largest sheet of water enclosed as a dock for shipping of heavy tonnage in the kingdom. Consequently, upon so large an export trade, the trustees contemplate making suitable provision for an export trade, and are prepared to appropriate a large portion of the North end of East Dock for public quays and warehouses, with suitable roads and railways, by which the greatest facilities will be given to the trade of the town, and the districts having communication by means of the railways.'

The opening of the completed Bute East Dock was reported in the *Illustrated London News* on 1 October 1859:

'The extension of this stupendous work was completed on the 1st of September and Wednesday the 14th ult was fixed upon as the day of opening. Preparations on an extensive scale had been made for the due celebration of an event as of so much importance to the town and port of Cardiff; but owing to the sudden death of Lord James Stuart – who for so many years had represented the boroughs of Cardiff, Cowbridge and Llantrisant in Parliament, and who was the maternal uncle of the young Marquis of Bute, under whose auspices the opening of the dock was to be inaugurated – the intended festivities were dispensed with, and the dock was opened for trade in the quietest possible manner. We extract from the *Cardiff and Merthyr Guardian* some particulars of the opening ceremony, and of the capacity of the dock.

The formal opening took place on Wednesday the 14 ult. About 12 o'clock the Marquis, accompanied by his trustees, the Right Honourable James Stuart Wortley and John Boyle, Esq, Miss Boyle, Miss E. Boyle, and Mr Carter, his Lordship's tutor, arrived at the dock in his Marchioness's private carriage, and proceeded to the office of the resident engineer, Mr McConnochie, situated on the west quay, where, boats being in readiness, they embarked for the *United States*, a steamer, the property of the Bute Dock Steam Towing Company, which was lying on the east side, ready to tow into the Extension the British barque *Maninidlo*, which had just arrived to take in a cargo of coals. After a pleasant ride across the dock in boats, the select party boarded the *United States*, where a limited number of gentlemen interested in the success of the undertaking were awaiting their arrival. Steam being up, the *United States* commenced her peaceful errand of conducting the *Maninidlo* into the Extension, amid the hearty cheers of those on board, and of taking her round to the west side, where she was moored to discharge her ballast. The *United States* then proceeded with her distinguished party down to the dock gates, and afterwards returned to the top of the dock, where the Marquis and his party disembarked and entered the family carriage amid the enthusiastic cheers of the few who, having heard of the intended formal opening, had hastened to the spot.

At the same time that the dock was entered by *United States* and the *Maninidlo*, the new canal which forms a junction with the Bute West Dock and the Glamorgan Ship Canal, was opened by one of the Aberdare Coal Company's boats (No 267) with a cargo of coal for Messrs David and Toms, and an empty lighter, passing through the locks. With the exception of a small steamer belonging to the contractors for the works, Messrs Hemmingway & Co, which followed the *Maninidlo* with a small party, this contributed the whole of the opening of the extension.

The Bute East Dock was commenced early in 1852, the trustees at the time being the much lamented Mr Tyndall Bruce, and Mr Macnabb, and the engineers Sir John Rennie and Mr John Plews. The first portion, in length 1,000 feet and width 300 feet, was opened in July 1855. The first extension, 2,000 feet in length and 500 feet wide, was commenced early in 1855 (Messrs Walker, Burgess and Cooper being the engineers) and was opened in 1857. The second and last extension, of 1,300 feet by 500 feet, was begun by the same engineers in 1857, and completed on the 1st of September last, including a junction canal communicating with the Bute West Dock and the Glamorgan Canal. The whole of the works have been executed by Messrs Hemmingway & Co.

The water area of this dock alone is 45 acres, and the basin 2¼ acres ... [and] ... the depth of water throughout the dock is 25 feet. The Bute East Dock is thus capable of accommodating the largest ships in the merchant services. Fifteen coal staiths are already erected and it is intended to put up seven more, which will give, when complete, a shipping power in this dock alone of a million tons and a half of coal per year. The accommodation for shipping in the port of Cardiff is very great, there being besides the Bute East Dock, the Bute West Dock, the Bute Tidal Dock, and the Glamorgan Ship Canal.'

Bute East Dock Basin

Bute East Dock Entrance Lock was 222 feet long by 55 feet wide, and the East Dock Basin beyond it was 380 feet long by 250 feet wide and covered an area of 2½ acres. The Inner Lock was 200 feet long by 49 feet wide.

Like the West Dock Basin, the East Dock Basin lay between the Outer and Inner Lock Entrances. The Outer Lock Entrance from the Entrance Channel had a set of outer and inner lock gates. The Inner Lock had a pedestrian bridge across it between the gates. Nearby, as seen on the 1882 map in Chapter 1, there was a Post Office; the map also shows that the Junction Dry Dock between the East and West Docks is only partly excavated, with only powerful pumps and a set of lock gates separating this work from the water of the basin. However, the 1901 map shows the work completed, with buildings for an engineering works on the west side and a railway line crossing its lower end near the entrance gate. By the time of the 1913 map the basin also has a coaling staith on its east side, with a warehouse on the west side; this warehouse later became 'E' and 'D' Warehouse. 'E' Warehouse, at the south end, was another corrugated-iron building with one floor, measuring 36 feet by 34 feet, and was used for the storage of general cargo; 'D' Warehouse, at the north end, was also of corrugated iron with one floor for general goods, measuring 205 feet by 40 feet. Also located on the east side of East Dock Basin was 'Y' Warehouse, also a single-storey corrugated-iron building for the storage of general goods, measuring 80 feet by 16 feet. In line with the Inner Lock inner gate was the corrugated-iron single-storey 'P' Warehouse for general goods, 144 feet by 48 feet, narrowing to 21 feet (originally of oblong design, some time before 1920 it was altered to a wedge-like shape).

Shown on the 1920 Ordnance Survey map are two cranes, one on the west and one on the east side of the Entrance Lock inner gate. Also a lavatory has been erected next to the pedestrian access over the Inner Lock, near 'P' Warehouse. The railway bridge over the Junction Dry Dock entrance is by this time referred to as a swing bridge.

In a Docks & Harbour Authority booklet of May 1957 the Junction Dry Dock is described as 419 feet long by 60 feet wide. Work on it was started in 1879 by Messrs Parfitt and Jenkins, and it was opened in 1881 with caissons at either end, one of which communicates with the East Basin, and the other with the West Dock. In 1894 the lease was transferred to the Cardiff Junction Dry Dock & Engineering Company Ltd, from whom it was eventually acquired by Messrs C. H. Bailey Ltd.

After passing through this Inner Lock complex, we enter the Bute East Dock.

Above This hand-coloured postcard was printed by the firm of Stewart & Woolf of London, and is postmarked Bute Docks, Cardiff, 3 November 1904. In the foreground is the hand gear to open the lock gates, by now hydraulically assisted, and in the middle ground are some of the hydraulically operated capstans and a mixed rake of open colliery wagons; three seven-plank wagons are from the Black Vein Colliery, Cwmtillery, while another three carry the name of A. L. Hopkins. *Author's collection*

Below This is the Bute East Dock Basin coaling tip, on the east side, photographed looking south-east at 5.30pm on 24 April 1884, with a good supply of coal wagons en route to another tip, probably in the East Dock. The pumping house behind the tip controlled all the hydraulic machinery in Bute East Dock Basin, while the building in the right background is probably the Customs Boarding Station, with the cliffs of Penarth Head in the distance. *Associated British Ports*

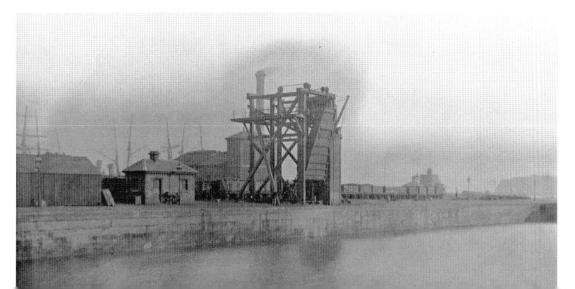

Left The East Dock Basin tip is seen again, photographed facing up the dock at 1.00pm on 22 April 1884. In the distance can be seen the tall masts of vessels in Bute East Dock, and a horse and cab. This is another good close-up of the fixed low-level type of coaling tip, and lying at its base are a selection of buckets that would be used in conjunction with the crane seen next to the tip platform. On the right a number of loaded coal wagons await their turn to be tipped. *Associated British Ports*

Below This panoramic view from the other side of the basin, looking north-east at 12.45pm on 25 April 1884, gives a clear view of the East Dock Basin tip, and its setting among the buildings that occupied that side. The tall masts are those of vessels moored along the north side of Roath Basin to take on coal. The pumping house seen here was located between Junction Lock and Commercial Dry Dock, but the purpose of the buildings in front and to the right of the smoking chimney has unfortunately been lost over time. *Associated British Ports*

Photographed on 10 May 1946, inside the Inner Lock en route to Bute East Dock Basin and beyond, is the SS *Sea Nymph* on her maiden voyage operating a new service between Cardiff and Belfast, operated by Messrs Patrick Thompson & Hoare. *Associated British Ports*

Bute East Dock

The Bute East Dock was 4,300 feet long by 300-500 feet wide, and covered an area of 44 acres with quayage of 9,360 feet. The depth at high water during an ordinary spring tide was 31ft 8½in, reducing to 21ft 8½in at high water during an ordinary neap tide. In 1882 there were 20 loading staiths with 27 cranes, and two graving docks.

Travelling northwards along the west side of East Dock in the 1880s, we would first pass an iron foundry (marked on the 1901 map as the Union Foundry, producing iron and brass). Next was a large reservoir and three coaling staiths with weighing machines; the second staith is shown with a timber yard on each side on the 1882 map. A second reservoir was then passed with only railway lines and mooring posts alongside the dock, but by 1901 the lines have increased in number and the second reservoir is referred to as the East Dock Timber Pond. There were a total of ten staiths on this western side, although the 1913 Cardiff Railway map shows that the second of the first group of three has been dismantled; a 1941

map shows that the lines to this former staith have been lifted, and an engineering works occupies this space. From entering this dock to this point there were 12 mooring posts (mooring rings on the 1941 map), which demonstrates just how numerous these moorings were along the rest of the dock. Beyond the timber pond the 1901 map shows the remaining seven coaling staiths, but by 1920 three have had their railway approaches disconnected and have been dismantled, leaving only six in use. In the early 1930s an extra one was built.

By 1880 the high-level coaling tips of East Dock were worked by the counterbalance system. A wagon of coal was drawn by horse power onto the tip's cradle; the shunting horse would be led off and a catch released, the weight of the wagon would tilt the coaling cradle sufficiently for the coal to shoot out of the wagon's end door into the tip chute, and from there into the ship's hold. The cradle had a counterbalance attached underneath that was sufficient to tilt the now empty wagon back to the level position. It was also possible by a series of manually operated winches to raise or lower the cradle. The whole process was safeguarded by the provision of brakes. However, a few years later hydraulic power took over, which obviated this manual operation; certainly by 1920 these tip cradles were all using hydraulically operated rams, with the shunting horses had been replaced by the use of hydraulically powered capstans.

Wharf Road West runs parallel with the west side of East Dock, passing beneath the lines leading to the staiths. Then come Messrs Hill's Dry Docks. In 1858 Charles Hill & Sons constructed the first of their two dry docks, the second opening in 1883 on the west side of East Dock. By 1957 the dry docks operated under the ownership of Messrs C. H. Bailey Ltd. They are marked as 'graving docks' on the 1901 map. No 1 Graving Dock (as labelled on the 1920 map) initially measured some 408 feet long by 48ft 5in wide; No 2 Graving Dock, to its south, was 400ft by 45ft. The wharf south of the dry docks was (by 1957) known as Sand Wharf, and nearby was No 7 coaling hoist or tip. North of the dry docks was Atlantic Wharf, handling traffic to and from America; located here were the grain warehouses of Messrs Dumfries, behind which was the biscuit factory of Messrs Spillers & Baker. The 1920 map shows six wagon turntables and three yard cranes operating around these grain warehouses.

At the top left-hand corner of the docks was a canal feeder, the Junction Canal, connecting with Bute West Dock and passing under Bute Viaduct, carrying the Cardiff Railway's lines. A short distance behind the viaduct was the LNWR Goods Station and the Tubal Cain Foundry, then, before the TVR East Branch, the Cardiff Railway Engine Works building.

On the top or northern side of Bute East Docks, in the centre, was 'A' Warehouse, with Bute Viaduct running behind it. This warehouse was of brick construction with five floors, and measured 100 feet by 50 feet; it was used for the safe storage and holding of bonded goods (it later became No 11 Bonded Warehouse). Running parallel with and behind the viaduct was Tyndall Street.

Down the centre of the Dock the map of 1913 shows 29 mooring posts, for securing vessels while awaiting loading. In the Depression of the 1920s and '30s many ships were laid up waiting for a cargo, usually roped together in batches of two or

three. Work was scarce and cargoes almost non-existent, and it was during that period that Cardiff lost almost all of its local and long-established ship-owning companies.

Returning to the bottom end of the dock, travelling north up the eastern side in 1882 we pass Junction Lock (which connected with the later Roath Basin). After the timber yard on the right was the terminus of the Rhymney Railway line, followed by the mass of lines that ran parallel with the dock; on the 1901 map two signal boxes are marked, one before the Junction Lock and one after. Once past the lock there were eight coaling staiths; between the first three staiths were three cranes, and from the third staith northwards were weighing machines working in conjunction with the staiths, together with numerous mooring posts all along the dock wall

On the 1904 Cardiff Railway map this side of East Dock is marked Import Wharf and warehouses, and, almost at the top of the east side, on the 1913 map we see 'X' Warehouse, another single-storey corrugated-iron building, measuring 80ft 6in long by 66 feet wide, used for general goods. A short distance northwards were three warehouses, named after the sons of Lord Bute: York, Stuart and Clarence. York or 'U' Warehouse was a stone building consisting of seven floors, measuring 200 feet by 80 feet, and was used for the storage of tobacco. Stuart or 'S' Warehouse was also constructed of stone, with five floors; measuring 200 feet by 80 feet wide, it was used for grain storage and general goods. Clarence or 'R' Warehouse was a corrugated-iron building measuring 200 feet by 80 feet, with three floors used for the storage of general goods.

After these warehouses were two further buildings, one a flour mill known as the Channel Mill, and the other a store. We are now in the top north-east corner of East Dock. To the east were the Cambrian Wagon Repair Works and the Dowlais Steel Works. In 1938 this side of East Dock was being remodelled as a General Cargo Wharf, which, when completed, would provide three additional berths for the timber trade. On the map of 1946 all the aforementioned coaling hoists on the east side had gone, the last two being dismantled in that year; by the 1957 map all of the east side was known as the General Cargo Quay.

By 1985 only Hill's Dry Docks on Atlantic

Wharf were still to be seen, and at the top of the by then land-locked dock stood the shell of 'A' Warehouse (the former bonded warehouse). A little further along Tyndall Street the former LNWR Tyndall Street Goods Depot could still be seen, with, in its shadow, the former biscuit warehouse, both derelict and vandalised. Adjoining them were the remains of the Rhymney Railway embankment and the nearby West Wharf Road, together with a few derelict brick, rusty-metal-roofed buildings and many acres of dockland that were ready for development, with more to follow.

Today the Cardiff Bay developers have turned the area of Atlantic Wharf into a showpiece marina.

Right This rather sorry-looking vessel is HMS *Hamedryad*, which was used for many years from 1 November 1866 as a seamen's hospital ship, until replaced by the Royal Hamedryad Seamen's Hospital at Plymouth, opened in 1905. She was subsequently towed from Plymouth and berthed at Bute East Dock, and this photograph was taken shortly after her arrival. *Associated British Ports*

Below The *Terra Nova* is seen here at anchor on the west side of Bute East Dock, loading stores and provisions aboard for Captain Scott's ill-fated expedition to the South Pole; because a number of experimental ice tractors were used, as well as ponies, tins of petrol from the Crown Fuel Works were also loaded aboard the vessel while at Cardiff. This photograph was taken on 15 June 1910, the day of their departure. On 17 January 1912 Scott and his team reached the South Pole, only to find a Norwegian flag flying – Roald Amundsen had beaten them to their destination nearly a month earlier. On the return journey all five men – Scott, Captain Oates, Lieutenant Bowers, Petty Officer Evans and Doctor Wilson – succumbed to starvation and extreme cold, and died only 11 miles from the supply depot known as 'One Ton'. *Associated British Ports*

Top Today the only time a congregation of wooden sailing ships is seen is during the 'Tall Ships Race', but it was a daily occurrence less than a hundred years ago. This view, taken on 19 April 1884, shows Bute East Dock with No 1 hydraulic tip, photographed from the east side of the dock. During this period many colliery wagons would be fully dumb buffered, or partially so with spring buffers at the door end and dumb buffers at the fixed end, ie the end to which the chains were secured while the wagon was on the coaling tip chute being prepared for tipping. The sprung buffers reduced wear and damage to colliery wagons, especially during shunting, but the use of dumb buffers (also known as dead buffers) lasted right up to the outbreak of the First World War. *Associated British Ports*

Middle This is No 1 high-level tip on the west side of East Dock, photographed from a ship at 2.30pm on 22 April 1884. The coaling roads can be seen quite clearly, at the same height as the chute; the fully laden wagons only needed to be tipped and returned, involving a lot less work than the low-level tips. In the background can be seen the masts of vessels in Bute West Dock. The water in East Dock was always at sill level. *Associated British Ports*

Bottom Also on the west side of the dock, this is No 2 coaling tip, photographed at 12.30pm on 24 April 1884. Two vessels are waiting to be bunkered, and in the distance a pair of cart-horses wait patiently under the road of the neighbouring staith. To the left is an empty six-plank private owner wagon belonging to Cory Bros & Co of Cardiff, the lettering in the early style, using small letters. It is a very peaceful scene, with a solitary man looking down from the coaling road and two deckhands taking the time to watch from the deck of the nearer vessel as the cameraman sets up his equipment, thus being captured for all time. *Associated British Ports*

Below A Cory Bros advert from *The Maritime Review*, 4 August 1905 edition. *Author's collection*

Right Another tip on the west side of East Dock was photographed from the deck of the SS *England* at 2.40pm on 24 April 1884. All of these tips seem to have a lifebelt hanging from a hook at ground level, and also a small rowing boat secured to the base of the tip. *Associated British Ports*

Below No 2 tip is silhouetted in this view from the staging wharf, photographed at 3.15pm on the same day. Maybe the photographer realised with this and the previous photograph that the sun was going down and he was losing the light. *Associated British Ports*

Right Photographed at 10.30am on 17 July 1884, this scene shows coaling tips Nos 7, 8, 9 and 10 on the west side of Bute East Dock. On the left is a collier with sails furled, patiently waiting for coal at No 7 tip; London was a favourite destination for these vessels. Behind the tip can be seen an open coal wagon. On the extreme right, a larger vessel is moored at No 10 tip, also waiting for coal. *Associated British Ports*

Above This photograph of the west side of Bute East Dock, circa 1906, shows the preparation of the new approach roads to the coaling hoists. Most of the wagons in view are Great Western Railway open plank wagons, with one Great Eastern and a few private owner colliery wagons, from Llanbradach and Cribbwr Fawr; this latter little-known colliery produced household and manufacturing coal, and supplied the Port Talbot and Swansea areas. *Associated British Ports*

Below Some time during the 1920s new roads to the coal staiths are in process of construction on the west side of the dock, seen here looking north. The concrete retaining wall is complete, its whiteness in stark contrast to the dark metal of the older overbridge. Wagons are bringing up spoil to build up the bank, and wooden planks, possibly shoring timbers, can be seen lying around, ready for use by the contractors at a later date. In the right foreground a man up the ladder is checking one of the lineside lamps. *Associated British Ports*

Above No 4 tip is under construction on the west side of the dock, circa 1931, with Nos 3 and 2 beyond. Below them, on the running roads, is a varied selection of traffic, mainly for dock internal use only. However, on the nearest low-level line there are open wagons bearing the initials CR, NE and MR, and alongside them are shoring timbers stockpiled for use on the nearby embankment. In front of these timbers can be seen a temporary contractor's line used to convey the timber to this spot, with a large baulk of timber blocking the end, as well as side-tipping wagons carrying spoil to build up the embankment. At the higher level even more wagons are in view, lettered LMS, MR, GE and CR, using what will eventually be the running roads to the tip, but at present transporting more spoil for the ever-growing embankment. On the bridge a tent has been erected, surrounded by boxes and sawn wooden planks. *Associated British Ports*

Above right In August 1945 Ebbw Vale Colliery wagons await their turn on the full road leading to a fixed coaling tip on the west side of East Dock. On the metal platform of the weighbridge is wagon No 31159, an open seven-plank, while the weighman checks the weight of coal being carried against the wagon's dead weight, which is what is happening to wagon No 0747, an empty open five-plank. The wagon manufacturer's plate can be seen at the right-hand end of the side of No 31159, and the colliery company plate is seen on the fixed end (nearest the camera). Once checked, the capstan man will draw each full wagon forward towards the tip as required. The empty wagons then pass behind the weighbridge on the empty road, a gradient ensuring that they run clear of the site. *Associated British Ports*

Above This undated photograph was taken in the works of Vickers Armstrong Ltd, and shows the testing of the hydraulic tipping equipment of the 'Norfolk' digging-out appliance, which will soon be in use at Cardiff Docks. *Associated British Ports*

Above By 1945 digging out coal by hand was classed as the old method. The wagon on the tip is seven-plank open wagon No 1648 belonging to the Ebbw Vale Colliery. *Associated British Ports*

Below This coal-wagon-lifting appliance at Cardiff Docks, better known as a wagon cradle, is carrying a five-plank open coal wagon ready for discharging. *Associated British Ports*

These two photographs show the 'Norfolk' spade digging-out appliance being used on duff coals, hydraulically pushing the coal towards the end door of Ebbw Vale Colliery wagon No 51059, circa 1945. Coal has a tendency to stick to wood when wet, and this method ensured that the colliery owners did not lose any profit. The pictures show quite clearly what this invention was capable of, carefully watched by several men – this must have been both frightening and fascinating for those close by, as the wagon's total gross weight of 12 tons is lifted up with ease and the gigantic spade goes into action. *Associated British Ports*

On the west side of East Dock in June 1953, near the site of the former timber pond, is an 'S' Class submarine, moored at Cardiff Docks as part of the Coronation festivities; it is identifiable by its rounded conning tower and only one periscope instead of three. I am reliable informed by my brother-in-law Ted Darke that this is HMS *Solent*, a sub he knew quite well as he served on her during this period. If it is *Solent*, it was sold to the West of Scotland Ship Breaking Co and broken up at Troon on 28 August 1961. The white stripe at the dockside edge was a wartime safety measure, allowing dockers or sailors to distinguish between land and water, not easy on a moonless night or during the blackout conditions of the Second World War. *Associated British Ports*

This is the last of the coaling tips on the west side of East Dock on 7 August 1961, all the others by then having been dismantled. Luckily Michael Hale was able to capture for ever the demise of the coaling history of the docks and record the scene on film for posterity. Today, even the steelworks in the background has gone. In the distance a rake of British Railways vans can be seen, beyond a ship named *Waverley*. M. *Hale*

Besides coal, grain arrived here from all over the world, mainly from America and Australia. This photograph, circa 1930, shows the GWR's Grain Elevator No 1, next to the Grain Warehouse at Atlantic Wharf, Bute East Dock. This was a floating grain elevator, which would usually be moored alongside a vessel or wharf and was capable of discharging directly to shed or barges as required. At the base of the viaduct are some GWR internal user wagons. *Associated British Ports*

This is the Tubal Cain Foundry & Engineering Works, Cardiff, seen here under the ownership of Messrs C. H. Bailey, circa 1922. These buildings were located between the north ends of the Bute West and East Docks. *Associated British Ports*

In this view from about 1927 pit props are being handled. In the background a small truck is being used to move smaller loads around, on narrow-gauge rails like those seen in the foreground, beside which some pieces of timber have been stacked shoulder-high on cradles. The men have rolled-up sleeves and coats removed – this was hard, heavy and, at times, dangerous work. Lewis Hunter cranes are discharging more Scandinavian pitwood in the background. *Associated British Ports*

This photograph, taken in April 1937, shows American pitch pine logs being discharged at Bute East Dock, to be rafted to the timber float. This technique of floating storage was used for heavy timbers and lessened the risk of them drying out and splitting. Seen from the Inner Lock entrance, the vessel on the left is the SS *Lotta*, port of registration Esbjerg, Denmark. *Associated British Ports*

Above As reported in the *GWR Magazine*, a new timber quay on the east side of East Dock came into operation on Monday 12 June 1939, and 15 days later, on 27 June, photographs were taken of the new berth. It was located south of York Warehouse, on ground that was once home to the coaling tips. This is the view from the embankment carrying the GWR high-level section of the former Cardiff Railway, overlooking East Wharf Road and the east side of East Dock. The vessel on the right is the SS *Merkur*, which is using her foremast derricks to unload her cargo of sawn timber; usually these ships' derricks could handle a 5-ton maximum load. Ocean Colliery wagons, including No 4486 nearest the camera, are loaded with pit props. Another wagon carries the name 'Glenavon', and another the initials 'BB'; this belongs to the Burnyeat & Brown Co Ltd, which owned collieries at Abergorky and Tylacoch, near Treorchy. Behind them are internal-user wagons carrying sawn timber. *Associated British Ports*

Left Finnish pit props are being unloaded into GWR four- and five-plank open wagons at the Timber Wharf of Bute East Dock on 6 November 1945. From right to left, the first three wagons are Nos 2047 (four-plank), 202820 (five-plank) and 203669 (four-plank), and they are all marked 'For use at Cardiff Docks only'. Usually pit props would go direct to the collieries, but the use of internal-use-only wagons can only mean that the wood is destined for the pit prop storage area. *Associated British Ports*

Right Cardiff Railway District Map of 1913, showing the top of East Dock and the Rhymney Railway's Bute Viaduct crossing over to the west side of East Dock from Tyndall Street Junction and the branch heading to the east side. *Author's collection*

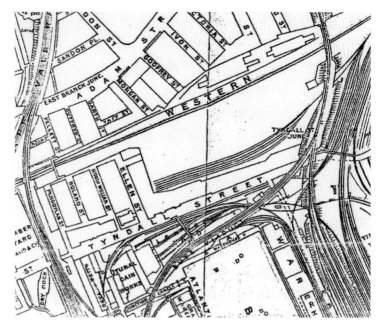

Below This view of the warehouses situated on the north-east side of Bute East Dock in August 1927 shows the SS *Hillglade* discharging bags of Canadian sugar by means of movable cranes. The clock tower of Channel Mill, although some distance away, is clearly seen, and next to this flour mill is Clarence Warehouse, then Stuart and, nearest the camera, York. The ventilated van bears the GWR number 85475 and, in front of all this activity, at rail level a man stands quite nonchalantly with hands in pockets, watching the cameraman. *Associated British Ports*

This view was been taken from one of the top floors of York Warehouse on 27 June 1939 (the same day as the upper picture on page 60), and seen at the bottom of the photograph is the corrugated roof of 'X' Warehouse. The ship nearest the camera is the *Merkur* again, and we can now see the exposed framework that held her cargo safely in place while at sea. The long planks of deal timber, having being discharged, are being manually moved to the waiting rail wagons, propped upright and secured in place; some will be stockpiled for later use. Behind the *Merkur* are the SS *Storsjeld*, SS *Kelvaldis*, SS *Skrun* and SS *Runa*. On the left runs East Wharf Road, beyond which is Roath Dock; seen on the skyline is the unique jib of the docks' floating crane. *Associated British Ports*

In this undated photograph of the Timber Quay on the east side of Bute East Dock, looking south, GWR bogie bolster wagons are much in evidence, with two GKN open wagons in the bottom right-hand corner. *Associated British Ports*

This photograph, dated 1946 and looking north, provides a good view of the unloading procedure for these long timbers from a Danish-registered ship. Planks are placed across trestles and criss-crossed for strength and stability, then, when ready, the deal planks are manually carried over into the empty wagons for stacking. On the right pit props are stacked high. In the background is the former Dowlais steelworks. *Associated British Ports*

Above Former Cardiff Railway engine No 3, carrying its GWR number 686, an 0-6-0T built by Kitson & Co in 1895 to works No 3602, is seen here on 11 August 1924; it was withdrawn from service the following year. It is pulling a GWR seven-plank open coal wagon alongside what appears to be a timber saw mill inside the Cardiff Docks complex. *LCGB, Ken Nunn Collection*

Below This is former Cardiff Railway engine No 8, GWR No 688, shunting at Cardiff Docks on the same day, hauling wagons stacked high with timber. This 0-6-0T was also built by Kitson as works No 3872 in 1899; it was withdrawn in 1926. *LCGB, Ken Nunn Collection*

Above This aerial view of the Cambrian Wagon Works, circa 1928, also shows East Moors Road running behind it, while in the bottom right-hand corner is Channel Mill, at the top of Bute East Dock. The Cambrian Works were wholly occupied with repairs to many types of railway stock, but generally to their own manufactured coal wagons and tankers. In the background are the buildings of Guest, Keen & Nettlefolds' steelworks. *Cambrian Wagon Company*

Below left A Cambrian Wagon Company Ltd booklet dated January 1928. *Author's collection*

Below The Cambrian Wagon Company was only one of several on the East Moors side of the docks. This advert is from the *Barry Dock Tide Table and Year Book*, 1891. *L. D. Bryant collection*

Right and below right All around the docks were small engineering firms that, in their own small way, contributed valued service to the people and firms that used the docks. In October 1985 these derelict and abandoned buildings on the east side of Bute East Dock beneath the former Rhymney Railway embankment will soon be bulldozed to make way for the new A4234 Central Link Road. The corrugated shed was latterly the home of H. & J. Welding, while the buildings in the far distance are part of the Allied Steel & Wire rod mills complex. *Author*

Below Taken at the same time, in October 1985, this view shows a little more of the northern end of the former Allied Steel & Wire rod mill; today it is the Castle Works site under the ownership of Celsa Steel (UK) Ltd, which became the new owner of these works and the nearby Tremorfa Works on 9 January 2003. On the right is Bute East Dock, with the clock tower of the Pierhead Building on the skyline and the high ground of Penarth Head behind it. *Author*

Above This view of the north end of Bute East Dock, circa 1968, shows the Customs Bonded Warehouse, formerly No 11 Bond and known before that as 'A' Warehouse. Running behind it is the Rhymney Railway viaduct that carried trains over to the west side of Bute East Dock (see the map on page 61). The arches were rented out to provide workshop and storage facilities. *Associated British Ports*

Below A sign of the times: on 28 August 1988 construction work has started along the east side of the former dock, which by now is landlocked. The former Bonded Warehouse is being converted into luxury apartments and the A4234 Central Link Road is under construction; part of this side of East Dock has been filled in to accommodate the new road, and the derelict premises seen on the previous page have now all gone. The large building recently constructed at the south end of the dock, and very prominent in the centre of this photograph, is the new Cardiff Council Offices. *Author*

Hill's Dry Docks

Above This hive of activity appears to be preparation work for the second of Mr Hill's Dry Docks, towards the top of the west side of Bute East Dock, circa 1883. A contractor's engine can be seen on the left, positioned under a beam fitted with pulleys and used for the supporting and moving of dressed stone as it is unloaded from railway trucks. To the right of the engine is a steam crane, which appears to be laying sleepers for another temporary line. Left of centre is a vertical-boiler crane, in front of which the ground is being excavated, part of it already shored up. The open wagons look like three-plank contractor's wagons, although the initials 'BD' may well be for 'Bute Dock'; No 728 is the nearest. Altogether three vertical-boiler cranes and two covered cranes can be seen, while the wagons look to be carrying spoil from the excavation. In the background is the top end of Bute East Dock, and the letter O in the diamond on the nearest vessel's funnel indicates that she belongs to the Syndikate Shederei GMBH of Hamburg. This was a transitional period between sails for wind power and funnels for steam power; most vessels had both, to save their coal supplies. *Cardiff Library, Local Studies Department*

Right The writing on the wooden beam states 'Sept 1st 1883'. The first of Hill's Dry Docks was built in the 1859 to 1860 period by Messrs Hemingway Brothers & Pearson, contractors for Bute East Dock. The contract for the second dry dock was let in 1882, and it was completed on 19 September 1883. *Cardiff Library, Local Studies Department*

Above On the opening day, 19 September 1883, the dry dock is filling with water while the steamer *Rhodor* waits to be the first vessel to enter. *Cardiff Library, Local Studies Department*

Below The *Rhodor* is now securely inside the dry dock, the 'caisson' is closed and the side timbers are in position, holding the vessel upright. These timbers will be lifted and repositioned over each step, or 'altar' as they are known, as the water is pumped out and the vessel settles. *Cardiff Library, Local Studies Department*

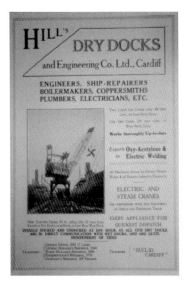

Above An advertisement for Hill's Dry Docks. *Associated British Ports*

Above right and right The *GWR Magazine* of 1932 stated that a new twin-screw tug, *The Earl*, had been provided for Cardiff Docks, 95 feet long with a 24-foot beam and capable of 800ihp. On 19 July 1951 the *Campania* entered the Queen Alexandra Dock for the Festival of Britain Exhibition, and while giving attendance *The Earl* sank. The *Margaret Horn*, which was nearby, picked up the crew and thankfully there were no casualties. On 11 September the *Ranger*, with the assistance of a floating crane and a lot of salvage expertise, raised *The Earl* from the floor of Roath sea lock. *Associated British Ports*

Right *The Earl* was taken to Hill's Dry Docks where she underwent refurbishment. The propeller will need a thorough examination, as will the engines, both clearly in need of an overhaul. During the war both Royal and Merchant Navy vessels that had suffered bomb or machine-gun damage were brought to these and the other dry docks in Cardiff, quickly repaired and returned to duty. Sadly it was usually the same men seen working here and in the other dry docks that also had the sad task of removing the dying or dead before any work could commence. *Associated British Ports*

Dredging

The 1939 edition of the *GWR Magazine* stated that to maintain an adequate depth of water at the company's ports, approximately 3½ million cubic yards of material was dredged from the channels and docks during the year by the company's dredging staff and plant. Earlier, in 1932, the magazine had reported that steam hopper barges Nos 3, 4, 7 and 8 were to be replaced at Cardiff Docks by two vessels of larger capacity.

Articles published in *Ship Ahoy* magazine are full of historical interest and I gratefully acknowledge permission granted by the co-editors Dr Don Anderson and Mr Chris Collard to include details here. In the summer of 1962 the magazine reported that the dredger *Hoyle* (1935, 3,145gt) had arrived at Cardiff from the Mersey during the week ending 21 April for various alterations after being purchased from the Mersey Docks & Harbour Board by Davies, Middleton & Davies. She was renamed *Sand Galore* and landed 3,000 tons of dredged sand at Cardiff, the largest single sand cargo to be landed at a South Wales port.

The following year it was reported that F. Bowles & Son, the Cardiff sand and gravel merchants, had recently taken delivery of the MV *Bowqueen*, a modern sand suction dredger, to operate in the Bristol Channel. She was able to carry 1,850 tons and could dredge at a rate of 1,000 tons per hour. A 1966 article written by Richard Pryde recorded that Bowles' dredgers were a common sight working off the sandbanks in the area of Flat Holm and Steep Holm in the Bristol Channel, and the fleet at that time consisted of *Bowstar*, *Bowline*, *Bowcrest*, *Bowpride*, *Bowqueen*, *Bowbelle*, *Bowprince* and *Bowfleet*, together with dredgers of two other concerns, the British Dredging Co Ltd and the Bristol Sand & Gravel Co Ltd, both by then under the Bowles group banner. These additional vessels were the *Dunkerton*, *Camerton*, *Badminton* and *Peterston*. Soon to join the group were the vessels of Western Dredgers Ltd, *Isca*, *Instow* and *Moderator*.

Bowcross was added to the fleet in 1971, being the former *Chichester Cross* (1967, 959gt) of John Heaver Ltd, Southampton. *Bowqueen* capsized and sank on 8 September 1965 during a gale while off Gunfleet Spit, near Harwich, with the loss of four lives. The vessel was subsequently raised and taken to Gravesend on 10 November, from where she

This is the GWR bucket dredger *Foremost 49*, circa 1946, used to maintain the depth of the dock entrance channels of each of the South Wales ports, and also to maintain the water depth in dock. When working she discharged her cargo into hopper barges moored alongside, which had doors fitted to the bottom of their hulls; when full they would open the doors to discharge their cargo of mud and silt down-channel. Today these bucket dredgers have been disposed of, and the work is undertaken by suction dredgers. *Associated British Ports*

was towed to Holland for repairs and refitting, after which she returned to service.

Harbour Lights magazine of June 1970 reported that the new £50,000 hydrographic survey vessel *Soniarus* had been officially handed over to BTDB in March. This twin-screw diesel vessel would enable dredging in the South Wales ports to be carried out with pin-point accuracy.

The Sand Dredger Wharf, Junction Lock, was at the south end of Bute East Dock. This is the sand dredger *Peterston* (748 gross/215 net tons), equipped with a five-cylinder two-stroke oil engine. Built in 1961 by Ailsa SB Co Ltd, Troon, it was owned by Messrs F. Bowles & Sons Ltd, Sand and Gravel Merchants. When busy these vessels would come in on one tide and leave on the next. The photograph was taken on 27 June 1987 from Junction Lock, with Bute East Dock in the background. *Author*

Rea's tugs

Ship Ahoy magazine also affords an insight into towage operations at Cardiff Docks. The autumn edition of 1963 reported that, from 1 July, R. & J. H. Rea Ltd had taken over all the towage work at Cardiff and Barry formerly undertaken by the Bristol Channel Tugs Ltd, who had gone into voluntary liquidation. Rea's took over *Royal Rose*, *Emphatic*, *Royal Falcon*, *Loyal Celt* and *Welsh Rose* from that company. *Royal Rose* became *Yewgarth*, *Emphatic* became *Hallgarth*, and *Welsh Rose* became *Lowgarth*. Rea's also purchased the tugs *Cardiff*, *Gwent* and *Windsor* from the British Transport Docks Board; *Gwent* became *Iselgarth* and *Windsor* became *Nethergarth*. The other three tugs were sold for scrap, *Loyal Celt* to Haulbowline Industries, of Passage West, *Royal Falcon* to breakers at Troon, and *Cardiff* to John Cashmore Ltd, Newport. The company then had a total of 21 tugs in the Bristol Channel: five at Avonmouth and Bristol, four at Barry, eight at Cardiff, and four at Milford.

Two collision and sinking disasters subsequently marred Rea's otherwise uneventful operations, and much press attention was naturally given at the time. On 14 September 1965, while assisting the ore carrier *Aldersgate* (1960, 12,718gt), *Yewgarth* was struck and sank outside the lock entrance to the Queen Alexandra Dock, Cardiff. Refloated a week later, she was taken to Newport and beached on the gridiron at Cashmore's Wharf for examination. Repairs were found to be uneconomical and she was sold to Cashmore's for breaking up.

In the early hours of the morning of 15 January 1966, while assisting the New Zealand Shipping Co vessel *Hororata* (1942, 12,090gt), *Iselgarth* was struck and sank off Penarth Head. Tragically three crew members were lost and the tug was not refloated until 5 February. Examination in the Mountstuart Dry Dock proved repairs to be out of the question, and breaking up was carried out during May by A. E. Knill, a local scrap merchant. The tug *Westgarth* was by then the sole surviving steam tug in the fleet.

GWR coaling tips

Above This view of the bottom end of Bute East Dock photographed at 12.15pm on 14 July 1884 shows two GWR coaling tips, and two idle tips. *Associated British Ports*

Below Trials between Welsh and Newcastle coal in Bute East Dock, involving the Bute trustees and the Taff Vale Railway, as reported by the *Cardiff Times* on 18 December 1858. *Cardiff Library, Local Studies Department*

Right This is GWR tip No 1, photographed at 1.30pm on 22 April 1884. On this normal working day the two men sitting on the coaling bucket are probably the coaling tip staff, while

the other two both wear what looks like bowler hats and are probably tallymen, or weighmen, whilst the person nearest the camera behind the lamp may be an assistant to the cameraman. The photograph provides a clear view of the gas lighting in use at this time; etched on the far-side glass of the lantern is a number, possibly 329. *Associated British Ports*

" This week an important trial of the Welsh and Newcastle steam coal has been commenced in the East Bute Dock at Cardiff. A screw-steamer, the Creole, has been moored at the east side of the East Dock, and the trial is now taking place on board her. Notwithstanding recent decided indications of preference for the Welsh coal, both by Government and the leading steamship companies, the Welsh coalmasters are determined to bring this matter to an issue if possible. Accordingly, two Government Inspectors, Mr Lynn, from the Portsmouth Dockyard, and Mr Tamplin, from the Woolwich Dockyard, have come down for the purpose of conducting and reporting on the experiments. In a question of such vital importance all who are so deeply interested at this port seemed to have joined heartily in subscribing the requisite funds. The coalmasters have subscribed liberally, and so have the Bute trustees and the Taff Vale Railway Company."

Another view of GWR No 1 coaling tip, photographed on the following day. Such pictures illustrate much better than words just how well-constructed these tips were; effective and efficient, they were the mainstay of these docks for many years. Beyond the horses and carts and the tip a partly unsheeted wagon can be seen, 'GW' prominently painted on the tarpaulin sheet. On the right a fully laden open three-plank wagon awaits its turn, its tarpaulin folded up on top of its cargo. *Associated British Ports*

This is No 1 tip again, at noon on 19 April 1884. The connecting track, the running lines to the next tip and hydraulic capstans are all in evidence here. I make no apology for including several views of the same coaling tip – accuracy of detail is important for both railway modellers and historians. *Associated British Ports*

The tip is seen again at 2.35pm on 25 April, this time from the water – alongside is the SS *Malek*. These types of coaling tips were ideal for handling railway wagons of up to 10 tons capacity, but when in later years wagons of 20 tons capacity were introduced the majority of these tips were made redundant. Also in view are at least three empty flat-bed four-wheelers. As already mentioned, the height of the water was always at sill level in Bute East Dock, due to the feeder dock and the fresh water supplying it. *Associated British Ports*

I should recommend engineers of steamers to always burn first, when possible, that coal stowed in the bunkers nearest the boilers, on account of the heat. This portion of the bunkers deteriorates more rapidly than the rest. Unfortunately, this portion of the bunkers is often left for consumption to the last, with unfavourable results.

When Shipowners are arriving at results of coals burned for bunkers during any given voyage, due regard should be paid to the quality and quantity of coals left in the bunkers from the previous voyage. Of course, the number of buckets of ash per day (that is, every 24 hours) has to be noted, although frequently it is not all ash that goes overboard, but a considerable proportion of small which ought to have been burned. The log-book should be carefully inspected, and notes made of daily consumption.

Above A more distant view of No 1 tip at 12.15pm on 23 April 1884, its large structure silhouetted against a background of open coal wagons. *Associated British Ports*

Left 'Methods of burning South Wales coals', from a GWR Ports booklet of 1927. *Associated British Ports*

Methods of Burning South Wales Coals.

Welsh coals are suitable for all kinds of Boilers and Steam Plants and give first-class results.

The coals are used very largely with mechanical stokers and with induced and forced draught, and it is claimed on good evidence that these coals give better results than coals from any other coalfield in the world.

All Welsh steam coals require to be burnt with thin fires. With hand-firing, to get the best results, the stokers should be instructed as follows :—

First.—Break up lumps of coal with pick and not with hammer to get as little dust coal as possible.

Second.—The fires should be about 8 in. in front and 6 in. at the back of furnace, care being taken that there are no holes in the back of the fires. Fresh coals should be added evenly all over the fires.

Third.—One of the most important points to remember in the stoking of Welsh steam coals is that these coals open out in burning and therefore must not be stirred up, and that thick fires stop the opening of the coal. The fires should not be stirred up, but when necessary raised up from the bottom with a pricker or bar from time to time.

Fourth.—Any fire-bars are suitable, but they should be from $\frac{1}{4}$ in. to not more than $\frac{5}{8}$ in. apart.

Fifth.—There should be a good steady draught.

Below From *The Maritime Review*, 4 August 1905. *Author's collection*

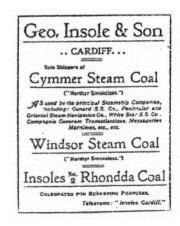

The Dowlais Iron and Steel Works and East Moors

Although it was from the shipment of coal that Cardiff Docks prospered, it was iron smelting that provided the foundation to the industrial life of South Wales and added much to the development of the port.

In 1769 John Guest acquired the Dowlais Works at Merthyr, and was to use the coal-burning method for smelting, replacing in an unprecedented move the older and less effective charcoal method. During the second half of the 18th century the production of iron increased, and by 1796 there were 11 furnaces in full production in the Merthyr area. With the rapid development of the railways the manufacture of iron rails in South Wales boomed, and by 1860 Cardiff Docks had exported 1,534,000 tons. From 1870 onwards iron was eclipsed by steel, so the ironworks turned to the manufacture of mild steel bars for the tinplate industry.

The iron and steel industry in South Wales depended on supplies of foreign ore, especially Spanish haematite, and by the 1880s imports had reached 500,000 tons. Declining local supplies prompted the decision to transfer the Dowlais Iron Works from Merthyr to an area near the Bute Docks, at Cardiff East Moors, giving the works the advantage of a dockside location, as well as savings arising from decreased of transport costs. On 4 February 1891, Lord Bute, on behalf of the Dowlais Iron Company, formerly opened the new works – claimed at the time to be the finest in the world – for the manufacturing of steel plate. However, the rail-making plant at Dowlais was retained.

In 1900 the Dowlais Iron Co amalgamated with Keen and Co of Birmingham, to become Guest Keen & Co. The following year the company acquired the nut and bolt firm of Nettlefolds, and became Guest, Keen & Nettlefolds Ltd (GKN), with its works adjacent to the parent firm. *The Railway Magazine* of 1908 reported that 'it is no uncommon thing to find that within some 60 hours of the arrival of a steamer, the cargo of ore in unloaded, conveyed to the furnaces and converted into steel plates for Admiralty purposes or general shipbuilding.'

Another amalgamation took place in 1930, when the firm became the Guest, Keen & Baldwin Iron & Steel Co. In 1935 £3 million was invested in replacing the by now obsolete Dowlais Works at East Moors with a modern iron and steel plant, alongside which would be the fabrication unit of Guest, Keen & Nettlefolds; in that same year the rolling mills and finishing department were transferred to Cardiff from Rogerstone, near Newport.

The Dock & Harbour Authority booklet of May 1957 states that the new firm

'...receives from Guest, Keen, Iron and Steel Company the raw materials necessary to feed

With the steelworks in the background, GWR 5-ton railway steam crane No 64 is placing long lengths of hollow box-constructed steel for storage until required at its final destination. Just to the right of the crane in this undated photograph is an embankment with buffer stops alongside a water tower, perhaps used for cooling steel in the plant rather than topping up railway engines. *Associated British Ports*

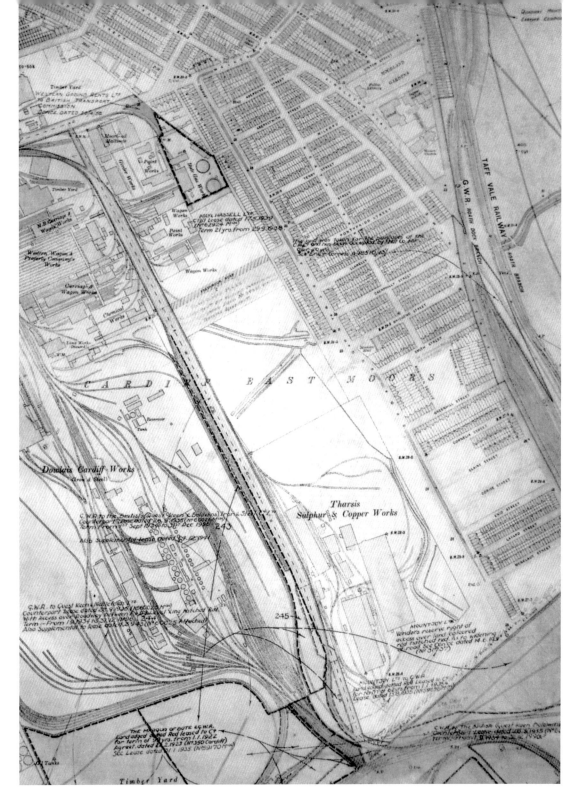

This map of 1920 shows the various agreements, leases, conditions, etc, granted by the GWR, and later the British Transport Commission, to tenants such as Guest, Keen & Nettlefolds Ltd, Guest, Keen & Baldwin Ltd (British Iron & Steel Co Ltd), Western Ground Rents Ltd, May & Hassell Ltd and Mountjoy Ltd. It also includes agreements with the Marquis of Bute, all dated. *Associated British Ports*

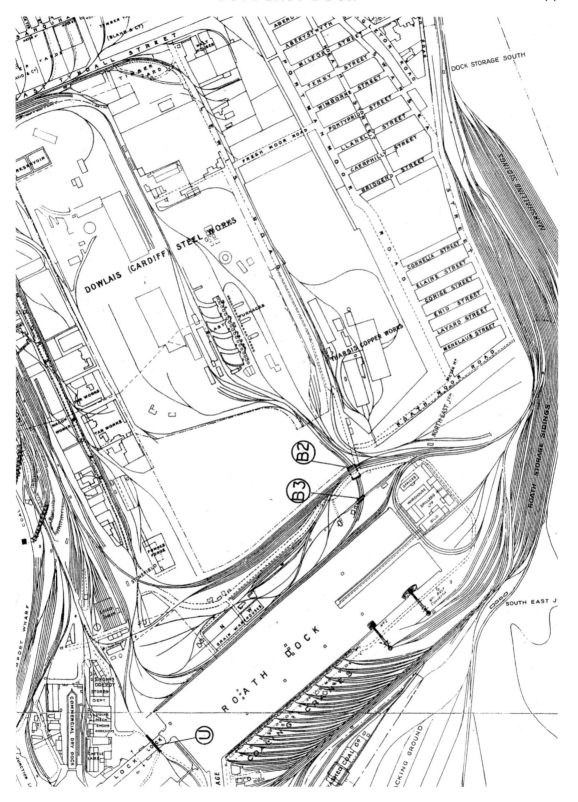

Ordnance Survey map of 1946, showing the Dowlais steelworks and Tharsis copper works. *Crown copyright*

its five mills, made world famous by their Iron and Steel products, nuts, bolts, screws, etc. These five mills comprise of a continuous wire rod mill (built in 1950), a continuous steel bar and strip mill, 12 inch by 9 inch steel rolling mills, a cold steel rolling mill, and a steel wire nail-making department…'

A new wire and nail manufacturing plant was added in 1962.

The East Moors Steel Works closed on 28 April 1978 following a decision by the British Steel Corporation not to accept any more imports of iron ore into the docks. The production of steel ceased and the blast furnaces, together with the rest of the East Moors Steel Works, were levelled in 1979. Many other well-known local works also disappeared as a result, and the Welsh Development Agency took on the responsibility for the clearing and site preparation of several hundred acres of land between Splott and the docks. Today the Ocean Park Industrial Estate, comprising many firms, large and small, occupies the site.

However, in 1976 a new rod mill had been built, known as the Cardiff Rod Mill (Castle Works), which, under the ownership of Allied Steel & Wire Ltd, produced high-volume quality steel rod at 500,000 tonnes per annum. During 1980 scrap metal was brought in by the road transport firm of R. J. Bird, which was crushed and dispatched to the nearby Tremorfa Works by rail.

Under the banner of Allied Steel & Wire Ltd, the several mills produced their own specialised products.

Tremorfa Steel Works produced steel from scrap, with a capacity of producing 7000,000 tonnes of billets per annum.

Cardiff Bar & Section Mills, Tremorfa, was a major manufacturer of angles, flats, channels, bars and special sections, in mild and high-tensile steel.

Castle Nails, Tremorfa, was Britain's largest nail manufacturer, supplying loose nails, machine-quality 'supa nails', and collated nails in a wide range of types, sizes and finishes.

Somerset Wire, Pengam Works, Cardiff, produced stabilised strand wire for pre-stressed concrete construction, high-tensile drawn steel wire for springs, ropes and the furniture industry, and general engineering.

Castle Wire, Castle Works, Cardiff, produced mild steel medium carbon wire and alloy wires for the cold headed trade, galvanised wire for cable armouring, both for land and submarine purposes, and wire for agricultural and general engineering products.

Carbon Carbides, Castle Works, Cardiff, manufactured for the bar drawing and tube drawing industries, cold heading inserts, dies and punches, nail gripper dies, and other tungsten carbon engineering products.

In March 2002 the USA imposed a trade tariff on all imported foreign steel, which had the effect of making British-manufactured steel more expensive and too costly to produce, with the result that on 10 July 2002 Allied Steel & Wire Ltd went into receivership with the loss of 800 jobs in Cardiff. In November the Spanish steel-making combine, Celsa Group, one of Europe's leading steel producers, started negotiations to buy the redundant Cardiff steel-making plants (Castle Works and Tremorfa Works) with the aim of re-employing some, if not most, of ASW's former employees. On 9 January 2003 Celsa Group duly purchased the former steelworks and

This 6 March 1987 view of Bute East Dock shows part of the concrete running-up road that led to one of the high-level tips on the west side. The Rod Mill (Castle Works) looms out of the mud and dereliction strewn around, and beyond tall cranes are already at work rebuilding the former Butetown and its nearby docklands to make the new Cardiff Bay. *Author*

production restarted in June, consisting of a Melt Shop, Rod and Bar Mill and a Section Mill at Castle Works and Tremorfa Works. In 2006 Celsa built and opened a new Melt Shop for the Cardiff-based Celsa Steel (UK) Ltd, which consisted of a 140-tonne ladle furnace and dust collection facility. This new lease of life for the works has also helped Associated British Ports, owner of the docks, by providing new work to replace that which has been lost and allowing the Port of Cardiff to expand towards new beginnings and a new future.

The accompanying maps show the massive Dowlais works, their blast furnaces, plate mills and associated buildings surrounded by other industries such as rolling stock works – including the Midland Wagon Works, Western Wagon Works, Gloucester Wagon Works (established by 1863), and Bristol Wagon Works (established by 1880) – the Eagle Paint Works, foundries, metal-stamping and enamel works, soap works, timber yards, resin and tar distilleries, the Bute Gas Works and Fownes Forge, to name but a few. East of the complex was the Tharsis Sulphur & Copper Works, around which ran the Roath Moor Road. A little further east was the TVR's Roath Dock Branch.

West of the Dowlais works, towards the docks, were 'K' and 'L' Warehouses. 'K' Warehouse was of wooden construction, with one floor, and measured 106 feet by 100 feet, used for the storage of timber. To the north were the timber yards of Robinson, David & Co and Bland & Co, separated from the steel works by East Tyndall Street.

The Pierhead Building

The Bute Dock Company offices were originally located on the south side of the Merchants' Exchange Building, which opened in 1886, but on 19 November 1892 the Exchange was destroyed by fire, and all the early records relating to the docks were lost. However, some five years later the company's new headquarters was ready, considered by many as the finest building in Butetown. It was designed by William Frame, who had earlier been architect William Burgess's assistant and successor during the rebuilding of Cardiff Castle (in 1865) and Castell Coch (in 1874), both for the Marquis of Bute.

The Pierhead Building opened for business as the new dock offices on August Bank Holiday 1897. The general style is that of the Gothic Renaissance transition of early 16th-century France, with special emphasis on the entrance, the tower above it, and the corner, which contained the Port Manager's office. The most striking feature of this ornate terracotta brick building is its fine skyline, provided by an exotic array of clustered hexagonal chimneys, pinnacle turrets and gargoyles culminating in a fine castellated clock tower.

In 1897 the Bute Dock Company obtained powers to construct its own railways, connecting the docks with the mining valleys, and as a result changed its name to the Cardiff Railway Company. To signify this new association there is a large panel on the west side of the building decorated with figures of a ship and a locomotive between the arms of the old borough and the arms of the Bute family; beneath is the motto 'Wrth Ddwr a Than' ('By Water and Fire'), which can also be seen on the mosaic floor in the main entrance hall.

The Pierhead Building was to remain as the port's administrative offices until 1921, when, as a result of the Grouping of Britain's numerous railway companies, it became the headquarters of all the GWR Ports, which at the time also included the cross-Channel steamer services from Fishguard to Ireland, and Weymouth to the Channel Islands. The building's national role continued until nationalisation of the railways in 1947, although the building continued as an administrative head office for the South Wales Ports until recent years. Since then it has become an administration office for the Port of Cardiff, then in 1982 it housed Associated British Ports' Regional Property Department, South Wales, and also ABP's Property subsidiary, Grosvenor Waterside, the firm responsible for the restructuring of the docks and the development of the massive Cardiff Bay project.

Today the Pierhead Building is Grade II listed as being of special architectural and historical interest, a well-deserved honour for a building worthy of being the centrepiece of the new development, and the focus of this newly redesigned area, which is now known universally as Cardiff Bay.

Above This undated 'Dainty' Series postcard captures for posterity an excellent view of the entrance to East Dock Basin, with the open gates and the stanchions supporting their handrails. While one vessel is already in the outer lock, what looks like a fishing trawler is about to join it. What is quite striking is how well the Pierhead Building, the Cardiff Railway's headquarters, with its Gothic style, blends in with the other buildings seen in the background – a very different scene today. On the extreme left can be seen the Merchants Exchange building, which by 1902 belonged to the Powell Duffryn Colliery Company and fronted on to Bute Crescent. We then see the night signal tower, and to its right is the port flagpole, which flew the crescent flag. Then comes the entrance to Bute West Dock Basin, and to its right a lavatory building. To the left of the Bute East Dock Basin entrance can be seen the starboard flagpole, which flew the basin flag. Judging by the number of officials and dignitaries waiting in a long line of welcome, this scene may have been photographed on 13 July 1907. *Author's collection*

Left A consignment of coal from the Universal Colliery at Senghenydd, owned by the Universal Steam Coal Company, heads for the Pierhead Building, dimly seen in the thick background of sea fog, to supply the offices' fireplaces, circa 1905. The dock gates were located at the entrance opposite James Street – the notice just visible above the wagons, beside the gate, reads 'Beware of the Engines'. *Cardiff Central Library, Local Studies Department*

Above Judging by the amount of people around the Pierhead Building, this must have been some special occasion during April 1911. The steam tugboat *Eagle* is at her mooring and well secured, and to the left is the signal tower with its fixed light at the top, which would guide vessels in the channel towards the safety of the dock entrance; in daylight a flagpole on the west side of the entrance would fly the crescent flag, while the other would fly the basin flag. *Railway & Travel Monthly magazine, April 1911*

Above right A drawing of the night signal tower from the Bute Docks Regulations booklet of 1886 and 1887, showing the sequence of lights to bring vessels into their respective dock at night. *Associated British Ports*

Below This hand-coloured postcard, printed in Germany in about 1900, shows a rather more peaceful scene from a similar viewpoint, and gives a clear view of the imposing red-brick Gothic-style Pierhead Building. On the left is the entrance to Bute West Dock Basin. Below the night signal tower can be seen steps built into the side of the seawall to give direct access to the small boats moored below. *Author's collection*

Above A time for celebration: in a stiff wind the flags fly proud from a newly erected flagpole. Beneath the Union Jack is the Docks & Inland Waterways Executive house flag, then signal flags sending out their message clear and strong – 'God save the Queen' – for this is June 1953, the Coronation year of Her Majesty Queen Elizabeth II, and Cardiff Docks will play their part in the celebrations. In the right background can be seen No 2 coaling tip on the east side of Roath Dock Basin, and between the tip and the Pierhead Building is Bute East Dock Basin entrance lock. On the left window-cleaners are busy beyond the lamp post with the lifebuoy attached, which has a ship's lantern in place of a normal one. Standing beside the small brick building nearest the camera is a smoke-blackened brazier alongside a pile of abandoned ships' chains; this is one of two blockhouses constructed during the Second World War, the other being near East Dock Basin entrance. During wartime these buildings would certainly have provided shelter for not only the lock operators but also the Air Raid and Fire Wardens, who would have been patrolling this area at night; they may even have been used as a decontamination facility. The older mast beyond the Pierhead Building, by now well past its best, supports a ship's lantern. *Associated British Ports*

Left A close-up of the intricate carving in terracotta on the western wall of the Pierhead Building. It includes the motto of the Cardiff Railway Company, above which are the arms of the old borough of Cardiff and the Bute family set between a steam engine and a sailing ship. A few steps to the right of this carving, above the building's main doorway, are carved the words 'Bute Docks Company'. *Associated British Ports*

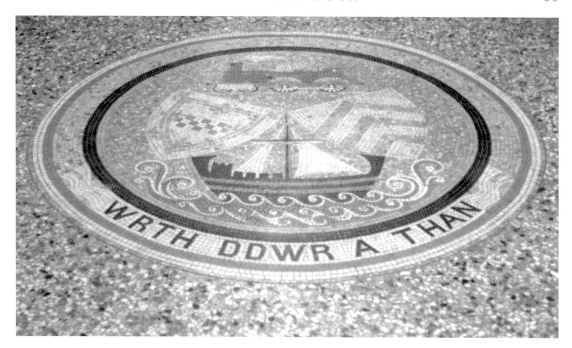

Above The motto of the Cardiff Railway Company – 'WRTH DDWR A THAN' ('BY WIND AND FIRE') – is seen again is this mosaic, photographed on 6 March 1987, just inside the doorway of the main entrance. *Author*

Below This is the Cardiff Railway Company Board Room in May 1971. How many influential and important people sat around that table, making decisions that would bring trade and wealth to the docks, and in turn make Cardiff the capital of Wales? The splendour of the room is enhanced by the grandeur of the terracotta fireplace. *Associated British Ports*

3. ROATH DOCK

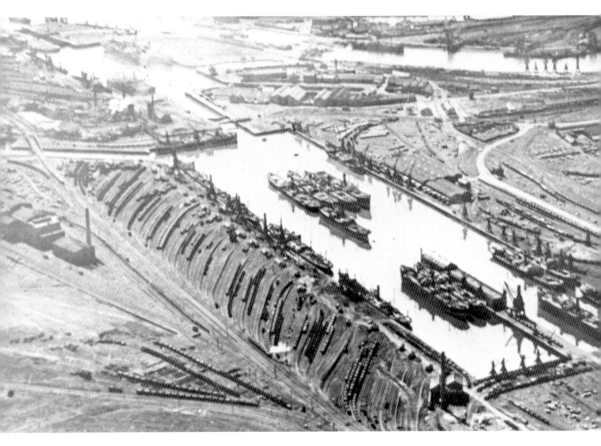

Above This aerial view of Roath Dock and its Basin was photographed looking south-west on 6 August 1930. Roath Basin is at the far end of the dock, and the entrance or sea lock can be seen at the far end of the basin, with Bute Dry Dock to its left. At the nearer end of the basin, on the right, is the Junction Lock and the Commercial Dry Dock. Next is the Inner Lock, with the cattle lairs and GWR engineering workshops alongside on the right. On the left of the lock is the Crown Patent Fuel works, and in front of them, like a silver ribbon, joining Roath Dock to Queen Alexandra Dock, is the Communication Passage. The comes the large oblong shape of Roath Dock itself. In the bottom right-hand corner is the area known as Pontoon Wharf, while further along the far side are 'N' and 'W' Sheds. Numerous vessels are berthed at the Iron Ore Wharf, while others are alongside the Grain Wharf. On the left of the dock is the Coal Washery, while at the nearby dockside coaling cranes are busy feeding ships' holds with good-quality Welsh coal. In the centre of the dock, and also in its basin, unwanted vessels are laid up, for work is scarce and contracts are few; their owners are awaiting buyers, and some will find them, albeit at a much reduced price, for vessels are going for scrap value rather than commercial worth. Of some 120-plus local shipping companies based in Cardiff, only a handful would survive these harsh times. *Associated British Ports*

Right This 1920 map of the Roath Dock area shows the various agreements, leases and conditions, etc, made by the Marquis of Bute, the Bute Docks Estates, Lord Tredegar, the GWR and the British Transport Docks Board to tenants such as Guest, Keen & Nettlefolds Ltd, British Briquettes Ltd, W. T. Rees, Mountjoy Ltd, South Glamorgan CC, and Western Ground Rents; all are dated. *Associated British Ports*

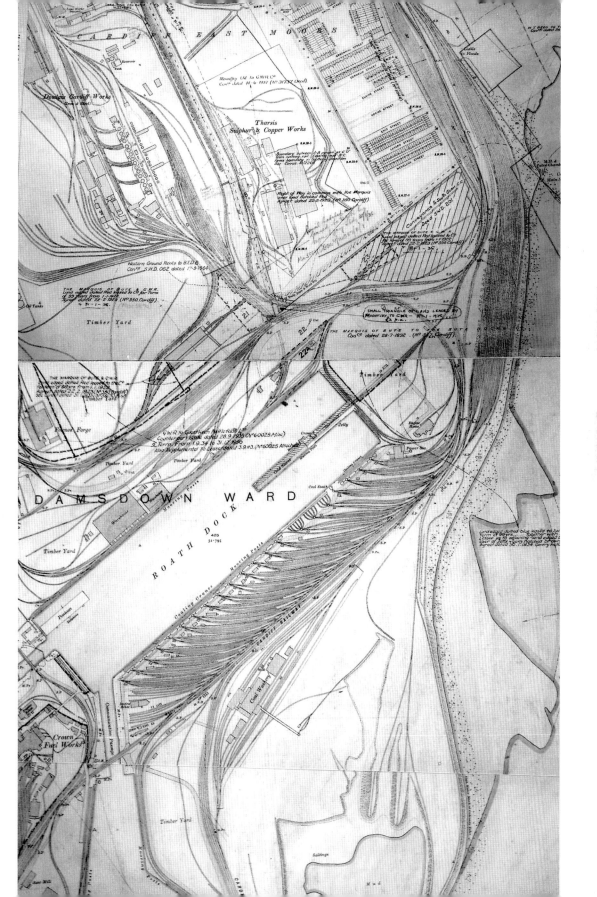

Left This second aerial view of Roath Dock and its Basin dates from circa 1955. Mountstuart Dry Docks are in the bottom left-hand corner – there was plenty of work for them that day – then comes Bute West Dock and Basin, their order books filled and plenty of work. At Bute East Dock there is coal for export, and beyond is GKN's steelworks, its furnace hot and smoke belching. In the centre is Roath Dock, her welcoming arms open to the grain traffic from Canada, USA and Russia. An engine pulling a train of more wagons than can be counted heads for the valleys, while another enters the docks, passing the endless sidings. On the right a vessel is at berth alongside Empire Wharf, Queen Alexandra Dock, and there is plenty of space here for the timber trade that was soon to come. *Associated British Ports*

Below Ordnance Survey map of 1901, showing the layout of Roath Dock Basin, as well as Bute East and West Dock Basins, the landing stages used by P. & A. Campbell's paddle-steamers, and the graving docks of Mountstuart Shipbuilding Yard. *Crown copyright*

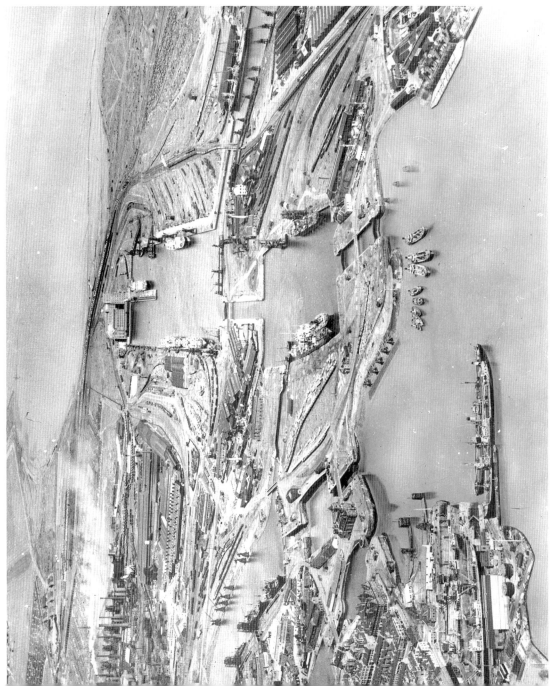

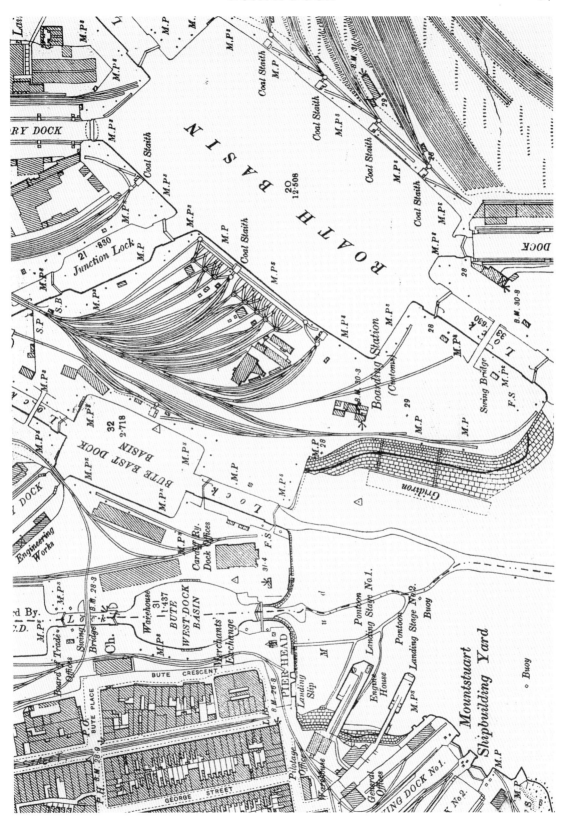

Roath Dock Basin

Although Roath Basin, its respective locks and Roath Dock itself were laid out from south-west to north-east, for simplicity I have generally referred to the 'north' and 'south' sides.

Construction work on the basin began in 1868 under the Bute Docks Act of that year. It was originally a tidal harbour, and much work had to be done before completion and opening on 23 July 1874.

The Roath Basin Entrance Lock was 350 feet long and 80 feet wide, and Roath Basin itself was 1,000 feet long and 550 feet wide, covering an area of 12 acres (some reports state 13 acres) with a water depth of 36 feet. At the time of opening there was a total of nine coaling tips here; by 1890 there were eight loading staiths and two cranes. The Inner lock was 600 feet long and 80 feet wide, providing a quayage of 7,920 feet, with sidings able to accommodate a maximum of 1,270 wagons. As early as 1888 electric lighting was introduced to the docks.

An 1882 Act of Parliament authorised the construction of Roath Dock and the reclamation of part of the foreshore, which began with the building of a seawall. By 1887 the construction of Roath Basin to Roath Dock via an Inner Lock was completed, and Roath Dock was ready.

Roath Basin was protected by an Outer Lock and an Inner Lock. The Outer Lock consists of two lock gates, between which was a swing bridge. The 1901 map also shows a Customs Boarding Station in the north-west corner of the lock area. Nearby was a gridiron (a frame of parallel beams to support a ship in dock), next to the dock wall on the Entrance Channel side; today this area is occupied by the Cardiff Bay Visitors Centre and the newly rebuilt Norwegian Church, which has been moved from its original position in Bute West Dock and is now known as the Norwegian Church Arts Centre. On the other side of the Outer Lock entrance, at the seawall, were 'dolphins', mooring posts set into the muddy floor of the channel.

Passing through the inner gate of this Outer Lock we reach Roath Basin itself. On the north side of the basin were numerous coaling roads and four fixed tips. These were later dismantled, and the roads then supplied movable coaling tips, which inaugurated a new method that dispatched

ships more quickly and conveniently. Two of the tips could load coal simultaneously into one vessel, and it is recorded that in 1920, using this method, 6,715 tons of coal was loaded into one vessel in 11 hours. In some cases it enabled a ship to sail before the tide had changed. By 1946 the map shows that these tips had all been removed, and by 1982 the area was known as Britannia Quay. Today the land between the former Bute East Basin and Roath Basin is occupied by the National Assembly for Wales.

Between Roath Basin and Bute East Dock was Junction Lock. By the 1980s there were sand wharves here, and the lock can still be seen today, although of course it is no longer a passage. On the ABP map of 2003 it is known as Junction Dock, and alongside it is the newly named Scott Harbour.

Beyond Junction Lock was another coaling staith of the fixed type (No 3 on the 1946 map, and removed by 1955), after which was the entrance gate to the Commercial Dry Dock. Built in 1875 by the Bute Dock Company, it came into the ownership of the GWR in 1922, and measured 600 feet long by 60 feet wide. New pumping equipment was installed in 1907 and gave very good service; its replacement was postponed by the outbreak of the Second World War. By then considerable difficulties were being experienced in keeping the pumping station open, mainly because of deterioration in the water-tube boilers, so it was decided that any new equipment should be electrically operated. The 2003 ABP map shows the Commercial Dry Dock as simply Commercial Dock.

On the south side of Roath Basin was the Bute Dry Dock and its entrance gates (still in place today). It was built by the Bute Shipbuilding, Engineering & Dry Dock Company in 1885, and measured 600 feet long by 55 feet wide, later widened to 71ft 6in. It later came under the ownership of Mountstuart Dry Docks Ltd.

The south side of Roath Basin also featured an appliance known as the 'Jumbo', which was a crane with a portable cradle on to which a loaded coal wagon was run and transferred bodily to the hatchway of the ship, where the door catches of the wagon were knocked out and the contents poured into the hold. This method was slow, but the idea was good, and led to the construction and eventual use of the Lewis Hunter Patent Coaling Cranes. By the 1880s these cranes were used extensively in the docks. The 1901 map shows four coaling staiths (reduced to two, numbered 1 and 2, on the 1946 map), and between them the ever-present mooring posts, still shown in place in 1957, but removed soon after, leaving the area as waste ground. By the 1960s it had been levelled and was being used for the storage of imported timber, then a new trade.

Above This view is from a vessel in Roath Dock Basin at 4.40pm on 13 July 1884. On the left is the GWR No 3 West coaling tip, then the entrance to Junction Lock. On the right of the entrance is the hydraulic power house, then another coaling tip and the tall masts of a sailing vessel in Commercial Dry Dock. Roath Dock itself was still under construction at this time. *Associated British Ports*

Below These two coaling tips, and between them an early type of coaling crane using the 'Jumbo' system, are on the south (south-east) side of Roath Dock Basin, and were photographed at 10.45am on 23 April 1884. Moored next to the coaling tip is the vessel *Amedco*. Everybody seems to be posing for the photograph! *Associated British Ports*

SHIP ON FIRE AT CARDIFF DOCKS.

About four o'clock on Saturday afternoon a fire broke out on board the ship Margaretta, of Bremen, which was loading a cargo of coal at No. 1 tip in the Roath Basin, Cardiff. It appears that the ship on her last voyage had carried a cargo of petroleum, and the fire originated, it is supposed, from one of the trimmer's caudles falling against a beam in the fore hold. The men at work had barely time to escape, and the flames shot up to a height of about 40 feet, accompanied by dense volumes of black smoke. The ship's bell was rung, and all the bells on the other vessels in the dock were also set agoing. Captain Frazer (the dockmaster), Mr Crockford, and a number of berthing men were quickly on the spot, closely followed by Superintendent Edwards and a strong body of the dock police. The flames were quickly got under, but water was continued to be poured into the hold up to a late hour to prevent any fresh outbreak A labourer named Rees Davies, who, with others, was assisting the police, was nearly suffocated and had to be hauled up out of the hold by a line. Captain Hofmann, overlooker for the steamer Prinz Alexander, also rendered valuable assistance on board the ship. The damage to the vessel is said to be very considerable.

Above This is No 3 coaling tip, at 11.45am on 26 April 1884, again on the south side of Roath Dock Basin. In the distance a vessel is being coaled. *Associated British Ports*

Left Pontypridd Chronicle, 20 September 1884. *Pontypridd Library*

Below A happier occasion a few months later, from the *Pontypridd Chronicle, 3 January 1885. Pontypridd Library*

Wednesday being the ninth anniversary of the birth of Lady Margaret flags were displayed on the keep at Cardiff Castle, and on the flagstaff between the East and West pierheads. Several of the ships were also decorated with bunting in honour of the occasion.

Right Four coaling cranes on the south side of Roath Basin in July 1932. In the foreground repairs to the Inner Lock gates are still under way (as will be described later). *Associated British Ports*

Below right A new 20-ton coal hoist is in course of erection at Roath Dock Basin, circa 1932, and the jetty foundations are in place for a second one (its position marked with an 'X'). Two GWR 'sheerleg' cranes can be seen, ideal for heavy lifts. The new hoists were necessary because of the introduction of 20-ton railway wagons as part of the GWR's strategy to use higher-capacity steel-sided wagons in place of the smaller privately owned wood-planked colliery wagons of pre-grouping days. These 20-ton wagons were the brainchild of Sir Felix Pole of the GWR. These hoists were fixed, so the vessel had to be manoeuvred to position its holds for coaling. *Associated British Ports*

Below The two newly completed coaling hoists in use in Roath Basin, circa 1934. *Associated British Ports*

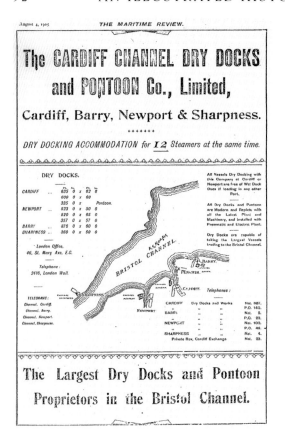

Above The Cardiff Channel Dry Docks & Pontoon Co was incorporated in 1897 as the Channel Dry Dock & Engineering Co Ltd. The dry dock was 630 feet long and had a 64-foot entrance. The company operated dry docks on both sides of the Bristol Channel, including those in Roath Dock Basin, Cardiff. This advertisement is from *The Maritime Review*, 4 August 1905. *Author's collection*

Above In the same issue was this report of labour trouble at the dry docks. *Author's collection*

FROM shipowning to dry docks is but a step, is it? As a matter of fact, the one is complement to the other, although it must not be forgotten that it is possible to run a ship without having a dry dock handy; while to run a dry dock it is essential to have a ship or two – unhandy, for choice? There is a bit of subtlety herein involved, if you have but time to hunt it up. We haven't, so we pass on to ask if you have heard of the labour troubles in the dry dock world? Labourers won't labour; painters won't paint; in consequence of all this, ships won't dry-dock. With the foregoing in mind, you naturally turn to the question of what you are likely to receive, as your share of the results of the dry dock manager's worry over the past half-year?

✚ ✚ ✚

WELL, it all depends on the particular dry dock which is implicated – or with which you are implicated, as the case might be. Some dry docks are inclined to pay very fairly – some ain't. With the latter sort, we are not concerning ourselves on this occasion – they'll come in, later on. But among the payers, we note that the Cardiff Channel Dry Docks and Pontoon Company, Limited, come first, with the interest on the "A" and "B" debentures, due on Tuesday, paid up like a shot. We have heard one or two envious individuals ask, "However does 'Billy Jones' do it, in these hard times?" For ourselves, we do not care to hazard a reply. If we were to give any sort of answer, we should have to state that he has done it out of earnings – bad times and all, notwithstanding.

✚ ✚ ✚

Below The full title on the boundary fence is 'Channel Dry Dock & Pontoon Company Ltd', and the picture shows a motor car being shipped to South Africa via the SS *Port Phillip* in January 1948. This was not a usual job for the company's 15-ton crane, even if the vessel was in its dry dock – it was a special arrangement, but one carried out professionally, with 'palliasse' bags against the car's wheels and sides in an attempt to prevent the lifting slings from damaging the bodywork. Meanwhile, in the bottom right-hand corner of the photograph workmen from the electricity company think about their work.

In 1963 *Ship Ahoy* magazine reported that fire had broken out in the motor tanker *Regent Falcon* (1959, 12,354gt) while berthed at Roath Basin on 11 October. The fire, which was brought quickly under control, was confined to the officers' accommodation and did not delay the ship being moved into the Channel Dry Dock on the 13th. *Associated British Ports*

Right The Channel Dry Dock premises in June 1987. *Author*

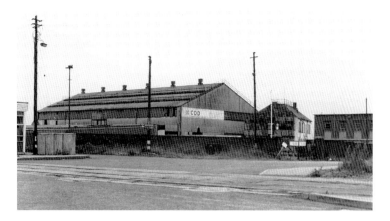

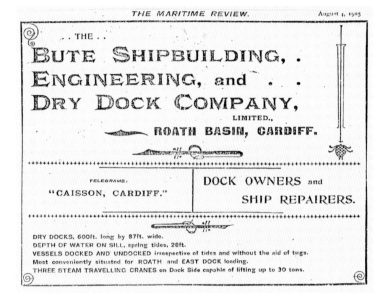

Left An advertisement for the Bute Shipbuilding, Engineering and Dry Dock Company Ltd, from *The Maritime Review*, 4 August 1905. *Author's collection*

Left MV *Hurunui* enters Bute Dry Dock in December 1951. One of the ship's officers keeps a careful watch in case of error – entering any lock or dry dock is an anxious moment for all. The water in the dock is 21 feet deep, and the vessel is riding high on a draught of 15 feet. *Associated British Ports*

Above Photographed from Britannia Quay, Roath Dock Basin, in 1987, during its period of redevelopment, this is the view towards the direction of the Bute Dry Dock entrance. On the right, in the dry dock, is the Shell Group tanker *Shell Trans*, port of registration Rotterdam. *Associated British Ports*

Left In about 1900 three wooden sailing vessels are held in the Public Graving Dock, Roath Basin, also known as the Commercial Dry Dock, which was owned by the Docks Authority and was available for hire. The 'windjammer' in the centre, having her hull scraped, is the *Serinner*. Repairs were just one of many jobs undertaken in dry dock – having a 'haircut and shave' was the dockers' slang for scuffing (rubbing) down and painting. *Associated British Ports*

Left This postcard photograph of the Commercial Dry Dock is postmarked 17 March 1906, and shows the *Sapphire*, of London, propped in place. The wooden props are held firm against the vessel's hull and the dry dock's narrow steps (or 'altars' as they were known), while her keel rests on the neat row of keel and bilge blocks. On either side of her keel are step-ladders and boards for walking on, which have been lowered down by the yard crane. The word 'Tydvil' can be made out on the wall of the large building beyond the vessel. *G. G. Jones*

Above This more recent view of the Commercial Dry Dock dates from about 1935. On the extreme left the gates into the premises are wide open and the word 'Commercial' can be seen on one of them. In the centre of the view a petrol-driven cement mixer stands idle, while the corrugated-iron shed behind looks new. To the right wooden posts, akin to telegraph poles, lay stacked close together, possibly for the stabilising of vessels in dry dock. The crane, newly erected, is a standard type of dockside structure, capable of a 15-ton lift and movable, a tremendous asset in this (or any other) dry dock. It carries a plate on the cab side: 'Stothert & Pitt Ltd, Engineers, Bath, Eng, Level Luffing Crane, 1934'. The two-storey range of brick building with the yellow engineering brick around the windows is the GWR's Cardiff Docks Central Workshops, and in the far distance, behind the corrugated iron shed, can be seen the ventilators and roof of the GKN steelworks. *Associated British Ports*

Right This was the view from Tyneside Road, facing the rear of Tyneside Yard and Commercial Dry Dock, on 6 March 1987. As can be seen the crane is still there, now 53 years old, and would stay there for a while longer. The sign on the wall reads 'British Dredging Ship Repairers Ltd, The Commercial Dry Dock Company'. The two large buildings on the left are the rear of the Tyneside Engineering premises (the GWR Central Workshops), while the building on the right was originally a canteen, but when it closed it was occupied by a private concern. *Author*

We now enter the Inner Lock. The outer gate was followed by a middle lock gate; originally the lock had three pairs of gates, but when renewed in 1932 the middle pair were not replaced. Then followed a swing bridge, which carried the Cardiff Docks internal railway system over the Inner Lock. There was then another set of gates, the inner lock gates, before we enter Roath Dock itself.

The *Great Western Railway Magazine* of 1932 included an article on the renewal of the lock gates at Roath Inner Lock:

'One of the most important works which the docks engineer is called upon to undertake is the proper maintenance and renewal of dock gates, on the strength and stability of which the safety of the shipping in the docks must depend. It is therefore very essential that the greatest care should not only be taken in their design, but also in the details of their construction, so as to ensure safety and efficiency of working, as any hindrance to or dislocation of shipping is a serious matter. At the Great Western Railway Company's Bute Docks, Cardiff, there are 22 pairs of dock and canal gates, which, owing to their constant usage, require frequent attention. Periodical external examinations are made by divers, as the most vital parts of these structures are below water and can only be examined in that way. The internal examinations are made by a member of the technical staff or by an inspector of mechanics. At the present time the renewal is in hand of the upper and lower gates of the Roath Inner Lock, which connects the Roath Basin with Roath Dock.

The old gates, constructed of wrought iron, were each 42 feet 6 inches high, 44 feet 9 inches long and 160 tons in weight, and were opened and closed by chains worked by hydraulic motors. They were supported near the mitre post by rollers, which travelled on a cast iron path at the bottom of the lock. The new gates are almost the same as the old in respect of length and depth, but slightly lighter, being 150 tons each leaf, and as the old roller paths are much worn, their renewal has been avoided by making the new gates buoyant, in accordance with modern practise, thereby dispensing with the need for rollers. This necessitated the renewal and strengthening of the anchorages holding the tops of the gates to the lock walls. The new gates were fabricated at the contractor's works, each part being fitted into its place under the supervision of the company's inspector, then taken to pieces, and finally built at a convenient site at Cardiff Docks.

The replacement of gates must entail some interference with the normal working of shipping, but the work is programmed to reduce this to a minimum. When the building of the new gates was sufficiently advanced, the preparatory work at the lock was put into hand. The old gates were removed by making good certain defects in the outside skin plating, closing the holes that normally permit water to enter the ballast tank, pumping out the water, and floating each gate away from its position after removing the anchor strap, which forms the link between the gates and the anchorage ashore.

In addition to the provision of the new and stronger anchorages previously mentioned, the work at the lock included the removal of the old and the fixing of new pintles or pivots, on which the lower end of the heel of the gate rests and turns, the building of the foundations and pits for the new direct-acting hydraulic gate-operating machinery, and the dressing of the stones forming the hollow quoins against which the heel post of the gate bears. These quoins are built of stones bonded into the masonry of the lock wall at the lower end of the gate recesses and dressed to a curve suitable for the heel posts of the gates. They are generally formed of granite, as are the ones at the Roath Locks.

There is always water in the Roath Inner Lock, and to enable the measurements of the worn quoins to be made, and the redressing done, as well as the changing of the bottom pivots, coffer dams were constructed for use at each quoin. They were placed on the floor of the lock, with their edges resting against the lock wall on each side of the quoin, the water being pumped out of the box so formed. To enable work to proceed at two quoins simultaneously two dams were built. They were 47 feet deep, constructed of timber, the joints being strengthened by steel straps and knees, so that they could withstand, with a suitable margin of safety, the heavy pressure of water, which, at the bottom of the lock, amounted to as much as one ton to the square foot. The joints between the covering timbers were caulked with oakum and pitch to make them watertight.

By the time all the work at the lock for the outer gates was finished, the gates themselves were practically ready, and early in August the first leaf was launched over the quay wall, towed to the lock, and stepped by pouring water into it, firstly to make it float vertically, then to cause it to sink until the socket at the bottom of the heel post of the gate was in place over the pivot. The anchorage at the top was next connected up and the ballast water pumped out. The remaining work consisted of coupling the gate-operating machinery, placing in position and securing the gangway for walking over the gates, and the final adjusting. The second leaf of the lower gate followed in the middle of August,

the gates were then tested for fit and working, and afterwards handed over to the dock manager for regular use. The upper gates of the lock are now being renewed in a similar manner.'

Twenty-five years later the Dock & Harbour booklet of May 1957 recorded:

'The Roath Sea Inner and Outer Lock gates have been overhauled and repaired in dry dock. An extensive programme of reconstruction and modernisation of mess rooms, lodges and offices has been carried out, as well as maintenance and repairs, and the making good of war damage to buildings, etc. The maintenance and relaying of railway tracks is a regular feature, involving about 170 miles of permanent way, and in addition the British Transport Commission is often called upon to undertake major alterations, due to projects promoted by the tenants etc, on the dock estate. Dock roads and crane tracks also fall for regular maintenance and renewal by the Civil Engineers Department.'

This new pair of lock gates were made by Messrs Armstrong Whitworth & Co for the inner end of Roath Sea Lock in about 1900. Work on the lock gates was undertaken whenever a suitable deep-water frontage was made available, then, when completed, the gates were launched into the dock and floated to where they were required. In the background are a mixture of various private owner colliery wagons: some belong to 'Llanbradach', and the initials 'HGL' appear on others, while over on the right a solitary wagon bears the name 'Hurford', of Cardiff. *Associated British Ports*

Roath Inner Lock gates under repair, 18 July 1932. *Associated British Ports*

Another view of the lock gates, as they are about to be launched. In the background is a steam-operated 'sheerleg' crane that will have been used to help with the repair and construction work. *Associated British Ports*

The repaired gate is launched; the next step, once it has settled and is floating, will be carefully and skilfully to tow it into the lock. *Associated British Ports*

Right The GWR's 125-ton floating crane lifts the lock gate into position. *Associated British Ports*

Below Another inspection of the Roath lock gates took place in 1954. The gates would be overhauled wherever there was room to do so, but more often than not it would be done in the Commercial Dry Dock, where shipwrights and other skilled staff were employed and direct labour was readily available. This photograph shows the completion of repairs to the west leaf of the Roath sea gates on 16 September 1954. They will have been completely refurbished and the heel and mitre ends fitted with new greenheart timbers, which had to be shaped to very tight tolerances. *Associated British Ports*

Below right One of the refurbished lock gates is being re-stepped, that is placed back into position. At present it is being held upright by the cathead of the fixed-jib crane mounted on a divers' barge; the diver can be seen about to enter the water on the left. At this period, 1954, the divers were equipped with standard gear – copper helmet, suit and lead-weighted boots – with hoses providing an air supply from manually operated air pumps, what can also be seen. The diver's air hoses are being laid out on the barge deck to enable him to traverse the lock bottom, from where he will guide the lowering of the gate on to its pintle (bolt or pin) hinge socket. Once in place the top anchorage can be secured. The building in the background is the Bute Dry Dock. *Associated British Ports*

Top The rendered building on the left was originally the GWR Port & Mechanical Engineers Offices, which was later to become the South Wales Ports Mechanical & Electrical Engineers Offices; a brown and white sign reading 'GWR Engineers' can be seen next to the doorway on the extreme left. The tall building behind it housed the boilermakers and blacksmiths workshops, while the three centre bays were the Cardiff Docks stores warehouse and garage; the remaining building and the lower ones beyond were the Port Civil Engineers Office and workshops on the top level, comprising a carpenters workshop and sawmill, with plumbers', divers' and supervisors' accommodation on the lower level. In this September 1984 view Tyneside Road runs in front of these now demolished buildings. *Author*

Middle These are the buildings at the far end of those in the previous photograph, seen on 6 March 1987. With the appointment of a Port Engineer responsible for all engineering disciplines, the engineering department was moved to the flat-roofed building seen in the distance, before being re-housed in new offices built at Queen Alexandra Lock. Behind the prefabricated building on the right is the high-roofed building that housed the blacksmiths and boilermakers workshops, at the rear of the stores warehouse; the prefabricated building was erected by a shipping agent as an office. Tyneside Road runs to the left of the buildings, with Junction Lock Road immediately in front of the camera. *Author*

Bottom Inside the Central Workshops in Tyneside Road a mortising machine is in use in the Civil Engineering Department in about 1954. These woodworking machines were produced by a number of suppliers; this one bears the name of Wadkin. *Associated British Ports*

Above Inside the Mechanical Engineer's Machine Workshops, again in about 1954, a hydraulic ram is in the process of being refurbished in a lathe. It was essential that the surfaces of these rams were regularly maintained to prevent deterioration of the seal through which the ram moved in operation. This ram could well have been part of the machinery of one of the many coaling appliances in use at this time. This building, with its whitewashed walls and 'No Smoking' signs, was a busy place. *Associated British Ports*

Below Turning a screw for a sluice paddle in the Central Workshops, circa 1954. *Associated British Ports*

Left As its name suggests, Roath Inner Lock Swingbridge, at Swingbridge Junction, spanned the Inner Lock between Roath Dock and its Basin. Looking north on 23 June 1987, directly in front is Tyneside Road and the former GWR Engineers Office complex. *Author*

Left By the summer of 1991 the railway connection over Roath Inner Lock Swingbridge had been severed due to land redevelopment and the building of a new distributor road. Steel traffic carried by rail from the Rod Mill's Castle Works, en route to the steel sidings between Roath Basin and Queen Alexandra Dock, now had to travel eastwards on leaving the Rod Mill, then turned north-eastwards to run parallel to the north side of Roath Dock, passing North East Junction to reach Splott Junction, then on to the newly built run-round loop installed in Tidal Yard before travelling south-east, then in a south-by-south-west direction along the south side of Roath Dock before finally crossing over Communication Bridge (Compass Bridge) to reach the sidings. This is the junction of Frigate Road and Tyneside Road on 23 April 2006. *Author*

Top A plate attached to Roath Inner Lock Swingbridge, photographed on 27 July 1987. *Author*

Left This photograph, taken on 23 April 2006, shows the MV *Seamark*, of Swansea, at anchor in Roath Basin. A retired pilot cutter, she is used by the Sea Cadets as a training vessel, and also doubles as their floating headquarters, having been handed over to this worthy organisation on 12 April 2002. She was commissioned in 1959, serving the ports of Swansea and Port Talbot until June 2001, when she was transferred to a dry dock at Cardiff before being handed over to the Sea Cadets. The Cardiff corps of Sea Cadets was formed in 1952, relying on donations and sponsorship, and the support of Associated British Ports in this presentation says much about the standards of the port today. In the background, still under construction, is 'Scott's Harbour', part of Britannia Quay, on the north side of the basin. *Author*

Cattle lairage

On the northern side of the Inner Lock was the cattle lairage, marked on the Cardiff Railway map of 1904 as 'Cattle Lairs and Chill Room'. Its buildings and pens were stoutly built for the holding of imported and exported cattle and the handling of prize bulls, operating under a licence granted by the Board of Agriculture. During the First World War this licence to import foreign cattle was extensively used for the importation of cattle from Ireland. Today the site is occupied by the Cardiff Bay Adventurer Quay.

Again, the *Great Western Railway Magazine* of 1932 printed an article on the livestock facilities at Roath Dock:

'...a few years ago the Mississippi river overflowed its banks, causing considerable devastation among livestock, so that for a time the United States took all the Canadian cattle that was available for sale. Lately the Canadians have resumed shipments to this country, and on June 2nd 1932 a consignment of 440 head of Canadian beasts were received at Cardiff in the Donaldson liner SS *Concordia*.

The vessels bringing cattle are accommodated in the Roath Dock, which affords facilities for the largest class of ships. The quay berth for discharging the cattle is conveniently situated at the south end of the dock, so that vessels lose no time in going direct to berth on entering dock. The Great Western Railway Company's cattle lairs adjoin the quay, and cattle enter the lairs direct from the ship. Here they are comfortably housed in the cleanest and most sanitary conditions. The beasts are individually examined by the Home Office inspector, in accordance with the regulations. Roomy stalls, giving plenty of light and air, with perfect drainage arrangements, allow the animals free movement, without being in any way crowded together. Suitable mangers and troughs are conveniently arranged for feeding and watering. The cattle are in the charge of experienced men. The arrangements at the lairs have been eulogistically commented upon by the various persons who from time to time have been engaged with the traffic, including Canadian Government officials.

Facilities are available for weighing live cattle on the hoof, and an auction mart, with a central exhibition ring for the cattle, enables sales to be conducted with despatch and convenience to all concerned. Adjoining the lairs are the abattoirs, into which those animals that are intended for immediate killing pass direct.

Railway facilities are available on the premises, so that both live beasts and carcases can be loaded direct to the railway vehicles. Chill rooms also form part of the accommodation, and carcases can be transported by overhead rail conveyors either to the chill rooms or to the company's refrigerated vans for railway travel. There is accommodation at the lairs for dealing with 900 store cattle or 500 fat cattle.

In relation to Canada, Cardiff is the nearest British port which can offer facilities for dealing with livestock traffic. Apart from the South Wales district, for which it is the natural port for this business, Cardiff can also conveniently deal with livestock for the Midlands, London, and other parts of England. It is understood that, owing to the intermittent character of the imported cattle business since the [First World] war, some of the ports in this country which were formerly equipped for receiving cattle have allowed their facilities to go out of commission. This has never applied at Cardiff, and the Great Western Railway Company has here a port which offers first class facilities for handling live cattle.'

In the same magazine the following article also appeared:

'A consignment of Rhodesian cattle, about 400 head, was imported into Cardiff Docks on Sunday the 28th of April, in the SS *Clan Morrison*. This was the first occasion in the history of the port for South African cattle to be received. The importance of the cattle facilities and accommodation available at Cardiff Docks was further emphasised during the year when, owing to the outbreak of foot and mouth disease in the Fishguard area, Irish cattle were prevented from being landed at Fishguard Harbour. The company's SS *Great Southern*, which usually plies between Waterford and Fishguard, as well as the vessels of the City of Cork Steam Packet Company, which run between Cork and Fishguard, were immediately diverted to Cardiff. During the time the restrictions against Fishguard were in force (August 30th to September 16th) there were landed at Cardiff Docks 1,796 cattle, 1,125 calves, 6,634 pigs, 440 sheep and lambs, and 14 horses. Thus attention was forcibly directed to the value of Cardiff as a port for the importation of cattle. There are very few ports in this country with facilities for dealing with imported cattle, and Cardiff looks forward to getting a full share of the traffic.'

In the 1938 *GWR Magazine* it was reported that extensions to the lairage had been completed and brought into use; the new building was 156 feet by 100 feet and could accommodate 300 head of cattle. The yards had also been extended and additional office accommodation provided.

Above The cattle lairs at Roath Dock in May 1947: the lairs consisted of an auction ring, as well as an abattoir and chill rooms. Roath Inner Lock can be seen in the foreground. *Associated British Ports*

Left Canadian cattle are being inspected as they disembark from the SS *Kastalia* at Roath Dock cattle lairs in September 1926, all under the watchful scrutiny of a GWR dock policeman and Home Office inspectors. *Associated British Ports*

Right The Canadian cattle slowly make their way into the lair. The photograph also gives a good view of the cattle boat, which shows all the signs of being a well-run ship, everything neatly stowed and the lifeboat held in place by its davits, its cover stretched tight. *Associated British Ports*

Below The cattle are now well inside the lairs, with a solitary man trying to keep them in order. In the background can be seen the cross-tree mast and shrouds of a ship in the Commercial Dry Dock, beside a sign suspended by wire, the reversed words reading 'John Rogers Ltd, Engineers'. *Associated British Ports*

Below right Friesian dairy cattle inside the lairage in about 1948. In the early part of 1950 the lairs were destroyed by fire. *Associated British Ports*

Crown Patent Fuel Works

North of the cattle lairs, and marked on the Cardiff Railway Map of 1913, were the buildings of the Mercantile Pontoon Co and the Tyneside Engineering Works. A little further north could be seen the smoke and steam from the Rhymney Railway yard and engine shed.

On the other side of the Inner Lock were the buildings of the Crown Patent Fuel Works, owned by the Crown Preserved Coal Company Ltd. These works were located on what is now waste ground, in the area between Frigate Road and the west side of Cargo Road; it is difficult to place them with any accuracy today because of their vastness when in their heyday.

The Crown Patent Fuel Works opened some time before 1860, and adjoined both the Roath and Queen Alexandra Docks, close to the Communication Passage. The idea for making briquettes was originally a French enterprise, first used in France in 1832, and was merely a utilisation of former waste material, the chief ingredients being coal dust and coal tar pitch. These were compressed by hydraulic machinery to form a fuel practically free from dirt and one that did not deteriorate either in very hot or very cold conditions. By the 1920s large quantities were being exported to the state-owned railways of Europe and South America.

Mr Glyndwr G. Jones provided the author with an insight into the works, part of which had subsequently become an NCB laboratory:

'I worked in the National Coal Board Divisional Briquette Laboratory for nine months, leaving in October 1948. The laboratory was situated in the Crown Fuel Works premises, and we analysed coal and briquette samples, the coal coming from a number of South Wales collieries. The coal was usually exported from Cardiff Docks, and the briquettes were exported to Ireland, where I believe the product was used on steam locomotives. The briquettes, or patent fuel as it was also known, were rectangular in shape and embossed with a crown; they were made from coal dust or crushed coal and pitch; this mixture was heated by steam in a pug mill and compressed into blocks, the pitch content giving the briquette a polished appearance. I worked alongside the Divisional Briquette Scientist, Mr P. V. Lloyd, who was 72 years old, who would often sing from operettas while he worked.'

The works was demolished in November 1973.

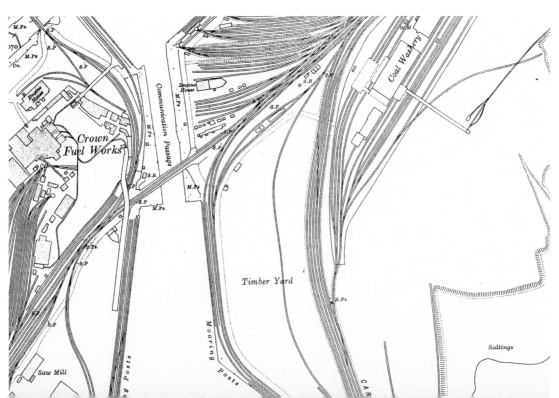

Below left This 1920 Ordnance Survey map shows clearly the location and layout of the Crown Fuel Works, on land between Roath Inner Lock (top left) and Communication Passage. It also shows the complex of railway lines to the coaling cranes along the south side of Roath Dock (top). Also seen here is the Coal Washery, and the nearby timber yard. *Crown copyright*

Above Patent fuel briquettes from the Crown Fuel Works are being loaded aboard the Egyptian MV *Star of Suez* in July 1951. Stamped on the sides of the briquettes is a crown symbol, and underneath the words 'Patent, Cardiff'. They weighed approximately 26lb each. In the hold it can be seen that the

briquettes have been removed from the wheeled trolley and stacked as tightly as possible. On the left is a Lewis Hunter 3-ton luffing crane, with the ladder giving the crane operator access to the interior of the crane and its cab. Behind it is a four-plank internal-user wagon bearing the words 'For use at Cardiff Docks only', and beyond that a seven-plank private owner wagon; the faded letters suggest that it might have belonged to the firm of Newbold & Martell, Coal Contractors, Northampton. This Fuel Wharf had been one of the targets bombed by the German Luftwaffe in a daylight raid on the docks. *Associated British Ports*

Above This view of 27 June 1987 shows the Communication Passage Swingbridge as seen from the south side of Roath Dock, looking west. On the extreme left is 'F' Shed, on the north side of Queen Alexandra Dock, and prominent beyond the swingbridge is the disused bulk of the Crown fuel storage silo and conveyor belt building, the last remaining structure of the former Crown Fuel Works complex, which was not demolished until 2003. *Author*

Roath Dock

We now enter Roath Dock. As mentioned above the construction of the dock was authorised by an Act of Parliament dated 16th July 1874, and it opened to trade on 24 August 1887. It was 2,400 feet long and 60 feet wide, covering an area of 35 acres (some records state 33 acres), providing a quayage of 7,920 feet with a high-water rise during ordinary spring tide of 35ft 8½in, lowering to a high-water level of 25ft 8½in at ordinary neap tide. The Taff Vale Railway's Roath Branch to the dock opened for mineral traffic on 23 April 1888, and by 1890 there were eight loading staiths and eight cranes in operation here.

On the north side, just beyond the Inner Lock gates, were more dolphins, mooring posts placed in the dock and tall enough to stand above the normal water depth of 36 feet. On the map of 1913 this area accommodated a pontoon, 360 feet long by 52 feet wide, belonging to the Mercantile Pontoon Company; this has gone by the 1946 map, but the area was by then generally known as Pontoon Wharf.

From this bottom corner almost to the middle of the north side were massive timber yards, and mobile cranes handled their varied cargoes quickly and efficiently. Some distance away was Fownes' Forge, hidden behind the huge stacks of timber piled up along the dock. The forge was located next to an area of land known as Stonefield, which was the location of the permanent way and coaling

A "BIG BLAST" AT CAERPHILLY.

A blasting operation of unusual magnitude was conducted at the Pwllypant Quarries, Caerphilly, on Monday, by Messrs. Mitchell and Scott, sub-contractors under Messrs. T. Nelson and Co., the contractors for the new Bute Dock, Cardiff. The operation took place in the presence of several gentlemen, among whom were Mr Farmer, Mr Simmons (engineer for Messrs Nelson and Co.,) and Mr E. Cross. The charge, which consisted of no less than fifteen hundredweight of gunpowder was deposited in a hole fifty feet deep. The powder was ignited by Mr Farmer; and after a lapse of twenty minutes an explosion occurred which displaced an immense head of rock. In rolling down the great height from the top to the bottom of the quarry the rock was broken into pieces, varying in weight from half-a-ton to five tons. The quantity of rock brought down by the blast is estimated at 10,000 tons, and the most remarkable feature in connection with the operation is that not the smallest portion of the stone was thrown upwards into the air. The whole force of the explosion spent itself in a lateral direction.

Above Blasting stone for the new dock: from the *Pontypridd Chronicle*, 5 July 1884. *Pontypridd Library*

Below Roath Dock under construction, looking south-westwards on 21 April 1884. Much use is being made of steam cranes with contractors' temporary lines everywhere. On the right are tipper trucks for the removal of spoil; the one nearest the camera is a front or end tipper, and behind are side tippers. Such wagons would not usually be fitted with springs, making them a very rigid construction, more akin to a medieval cart than a railway wagon. The tipping mechanism would be secured with a pin when travelling. *Associated British Ports*

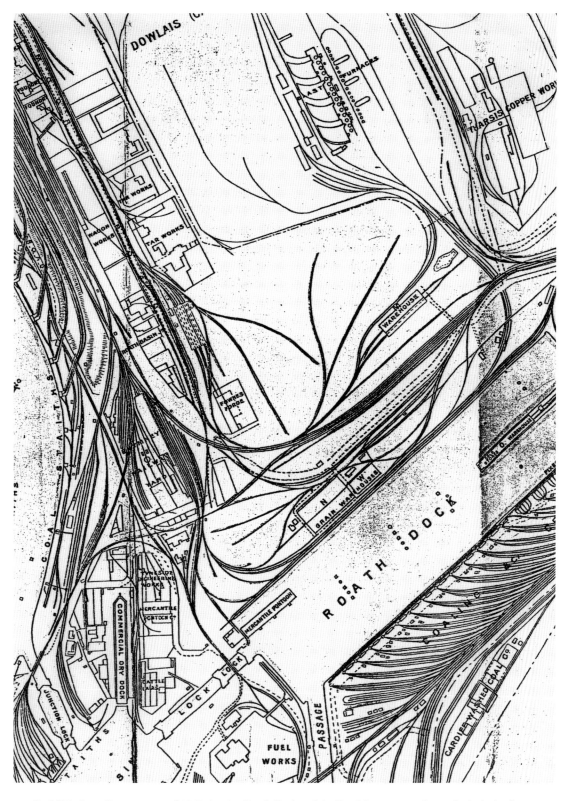

Cardiff Railway Company map of 1913 showing Roath Dock and the East Moors area to the north. *Author's collection*

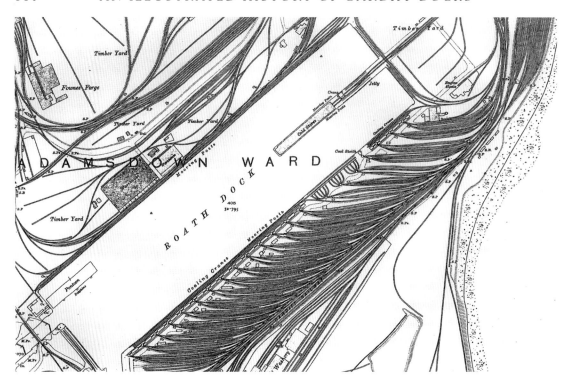

Above   Ordnance Survey map of 1920, showing the Mercantile Pontoon and 'N' and 'W' Warehouses on the north side of Roath Dock, the Cold Store on the jetty, the numerous coaling lines on the south side, and the huge areas covered by timber yards. *Crown copyright*

Below   An overall view of Roath Dock looking north-east, circa 1912, from a GWR Ports booklet. *Associated British Ports*

shed for the engines that worked the docks. On the 1904 map this area of dockside is marked as the Import Wharf, and the map of 1901 shows two warehouses at the centre of the dock, surrounded by the timber yards. By 1913 these warehouses are labelled as 'N' and 'W' grain warehouses. 'N' Warehouse was of corrugated-iron construction with two floors, measuring 300 feet long by 160 feet wide, and was used for the storage of general cargo as well as grain. 'W' Warehouse, also of corrugated iron with two floors, measured 170 feet by 80 feet and was likewise used for grain and general cargo storage. Today the quayside area where 'N' and 'W' sheds were is used by UMA Aggregates and Hanson Aggregates.

An unmarked road ran behind them (later this became Roath Dock Road), leading to an additional warehouse a short distance inland, at the Roath Dock side of the Dowlais Cardiff Steel Works boundary. This was 'M' Warehouse, of corrugated iron and measuring 300 feet long by 60 feet wide, its single floor used for the storage of hay and general goods.

The bottom south-east corner of Roath Dock would eventually be the site for the Communication Passage connecting the Roath and Queen Alexandra Docks, but at the turn of the 19th century there were only the running lines to the coaling cranes, and a line going to the Crown Fuel Works. On the 1901 map there are 15 double sets of lines feeding the coaling cranes on this south side; the cranes were by then the aforementioned

Lewis Hunter patent coaling cranes, capable of lifting 20 to 25 tons. However, instead of lifting the wagon, as did the 'Jumbo' crane, pits were constructed, and a large coal box was attached to the crane's jib and lowered into the pit; the laden wagon was then worked by capstan from the berth road on to a hydraulic kick-up, which tilted the wagon and deposited the coal into the box in the pit. The box was then lifted by the crane, transferred to the ship and lowered into the hold. An independent chain was attached to the inverted cone-shaped bottom of the box; when released, the cone spread the coal evenly in the hold with little or no breakage. Furthermore, the ship was well 'trimmed' and there was less possibility of an accident by spontaneous combustion, which might result from the accumulation of small coal on one side of the ship. Using this method also ensured that the coal reached its destination in a much better condition than when shipped by means of the ordinary tip-chute method. These cranes would also later be used in the Queen Alexandra Dock.

On the 1920 map there are four sets of lines to each of 14 coaling cranes, then three sets of three lines leading to the movable coaling staith; the map also shows that these lines have increased in number dramatically. Beyond them was a solitary coaling staith (in position on the 1901 map).

At the topmost end of the south side of the dock were another four sets of double lines going to the coaling cranes situated there; these had been

Roath Dock seen from the floating pontoon of the Mercantile Pontoon Company, circa 1908. The advertisement is from *The Maritime Review* of 4 August 1905. *The Railway Magazine, July 1908/Associated British Ports*

reduced to three by 1904, and by 1913 all the coaling cranes along this side of Roath Dock were shown as belonging to Coaling Cranes & Co.

Once again, the *Great Western Railway Magazine* of 1932 gives fascinating details under the heading 'Improvements at the South Wales Docks':

'Though the traffic position has been discouraging, the Great Western Railway Company have continued their general policy of maintaining the highest standard of facilities and equipment of the docks, and providing new appliances. The following is a brief description of improvements, alterations, and new works which have been completed or are at present in hand at the docks…

Twelve new 3-ton electric luffing cranes have been provided at Queen Alexandra Dock, and one 3-ton electric luffing crane at Roath Dock.

Two most useful new 20-ton traverser hoists have been erected at the northern end of Queen Alexandra Dock, and brought into commission.

A further three similar hoists are now in course of erection. These will be completed and ready for use early in 1932. A new 20-ton

fixed hoist is also in course of erection at the East Bute Dock, Cardiff.

The coal shipping facilities at the Roath Dock are being considerably improved and it has been decided to install belt conveyors of the most modern design. Work is nearing completion on the first of these appliances.'

Under the heading 'New Steamship Lines' the report continues:

'The Company's docks offer many advantages to the ship-owner in the way of low tonnage dues, special bunkering facilities, quick turn-round of vessels, and good prospects for outward cargoes of coal and steel. These advantages, together with the excellent dock facilities, continue to attract new steamship lines to call at the South Wales docks. A new line was inaugurated when Messrs W. R. Smith & Sons Ltd, Cardiff, commenced a service between the Pacific ports and South Wales, and the first call was made by the SS *Indian City* at Penarth Dock in December 1930. This vessel was followed by the *Quebec City* at Cardiff Docks on January 17th 1931, and since that date vessels have called at Cardiff Docks at regular intervals.'

Below left Roath Dock opened on 24 August 1887, but it was some eights months before coal traffic on the Roath Branch of the Taff Vale Railway reached it, on 23 April 1888. It is hard to realise that this bare-looking dock would grow into the busy and prosperous facility it became. Two early Lewis Hunter coaling cranes – identified by the wide archway between the legs – can be seen. *Associated British Ports*

Above Lewis Hunter coaling cranes are seen at Roath Dock in about 1905. Hydraulically operated, they had luffing capabilities but were too cumbersome for cargo operations; although they would be used as a crane for occasional lifts, they were designed specifically for coal-loading operations. Note the 'Despatch' anti-breakage boxes, one on a wheeled trolley and other being lifted by the crane. *Associated British Ports*

Above right This later scene, circa 1925, gives us a good view of the 'Despatch' anti-breakage box, as described in the text, its cone lowered. When discharging, the coal would be dispersed by the cone around the hold as the box was raised upwards on its return journey. Nearer the camera is a box waiting on its wheeled trolley. Beyond the crane are some five-plank open private owner wagons. The last of these Lewis Hunter cranes were dismantled in 1958. *Associated British Ports*

Right In another busy scene at Roath Dock circa 1925, at the base of the crane a coal wagon is being prepared to drop its coal into the waiting anti-breakage box in the pit below. Next to the weighbridge hut a young lad stands with his bicycle, which from the turn of the last century was a favourite means of transport, especially among the working class, as it was better than walking. *Associated British Ports*

Left Another view of shipping coal into the box of a Lewis Hunter coaling crane at Roath Dock, circa 1905. One man holds a hammer to release the pins holding the wagon's end doors, while another pulls the lever operating the hydraulic ramp. *The Railway Magazine, 1908*

Trimming Charges on Steamers and Sailers.

(National Coal Trimming Tariff.)

NOTE.—All rates in this Tariff are subject to 40 per cent reduction from January 1st, 1927.

Cargo Trimming Tariff.

(STEAMERS.)

1.	Single-deck vessels	6d. per ton.
2.	Two-deck vessels	8d. ,,
3.	Three-deck vessels	10½d. ,,
4.	Four-deck vessels	1s. 1d. ,,

not exceeding 20 feet from coamings to bulkhead.

5. Over-distances.—When distance exceeds 20 feet, the following rates to be paid, in addition to tariff rates, on all coal shipped in the hold where over-distance occurs :—

Vessels of 1 and 2 decks are to pay as under :—

(*a*) Cargoes of 500 tons and under :—If normal, according to Schedule. If abnormal, to be settled by agreement.

(*b*) Over 500 tons and up to 1,500 tons deadweight cargo :—

Over 20 feet and not exceeding	26 feet	1d. per ton.
,, 26 ,, ,, ,,	30 ,, ...	2d. ,,
,, 30 ,, ,, ,,	34 ,, ...	3½d. ,,
,, 34 ,, ,, ,,	38 ,, ...	4½d. ,,
,, 38 ,, ,, ,,	40 ,, ...	5d. ,,

(*c*) Over 1,500 tons deadweight cargo :—

Over 20 feet and not exceeding	26 feet	¾d. per ton.
,, 26 ,, ,, ,,	30 ,, ...	1½d. ,,
,, 30 ,, ,, ,,	34 ,, ...	2½d. ,,
,, 34 ,, ,, ,,	38 ,, ...	3½d. ,,
,, 38 ,, ,, ,,	40 ,, ...	4½d. ,,

Vessels of 3 and 4 decks are to pay as under :—

(*d*) Over 20 feet and not exceeding 26 feet .. .. 1d. per ton.

,, 26 ,, ,, ,,	30 ,, ...	1¾d. ,,
,, 30 ,, ,, ,,	34 ,, ...	2¾d. ,,
,, 34 ,, ,, ,,	38 ,, ...	3¾d. ,,
,, 38 ,, ,, ,,	40 ,, ...	4¾d. ,,

Where there is sufficient capacity in an end hold to enable the coal to be trimmed by a single cast or heave, no over-distance shall be paid whatever may be length of the ends, provided that notice is given in advance that only one heave is required. Agreed December, 1926.

These rates to apply to all coals shipped in 'tween-decks and lower holds, whether the long end occurs in both ends or in one only.

6. One-deck Steamers with Extended Bridge Decks, Awning Decks, or Shelter Decks.—For the holds covered by such decks, 7d. per ton, provided that when cargo is required to be trimmed on the main deck of these steamers, the two-deck rate of 8d. per ton is to be paid on all coal shipped into such holds.

Left Coal trimming charges on steamers and sailing ships, from a GWR docks booklet of 1927. *Associated British Ports*

Below From *The Maritime Review*, 4 August 1905. *Author's collection*

Right Vessels berthed beside the Lewis Hunter coaling cranes at Roath Dock in about 1920, from a 1922 GWR Ports booklet. *Associated British Ports*

Above This similar view dates from about 1930. All kinds of vessels are to be seen, but all with one purpose: to take on good Welsh coal and carry it around the world. The sad aspect of this view is that the vessels on the left are lashed together and secured by ropes, awaiting the fate that fell upon men and ships alike in that age of the great Depression: to be made redundant and thrown on the scrap heap. In 1938 the *GWR Magazine* reported that the feed roads to the coaling cranes at Roath Dock were being overhauled and new weighing facilities provided – but perhaps it was a case of acting too late, for change was on its way. *Associated British Ports*

Right With the new Belt Conveyor on the south side of Roath Dock in the background, a visit by senior dock and shipping representatives is taking place on 1 August 1934, possibly to mark the inauguration of a new coal export agreement. *Associated British Ports*

Above One of the two awesome Belt Conveyors, the second to be built, is seen in May 1936, and both were capable of handling 20-ton wagons. This rear view shows the enclosed feed belt leading to the impressive construction of latticework. On the extreme right, dwarfed by the structure, is either a Bedford or Chevrolet open pick-up truck belonging to a firm of manufacturing engineers. *Associated British Ports*

Below The two Belt Conveyors at the top end of the south side of Roath Dock in action in about 1937. *Associated British Ports*

The south side of Roath Dock was used for many years as a timber storage area. Photographed in about 1927, the three-plank open wagon is yet another internal-user vehicle. On the right can be seen the goose-necked jib of the floating crane, while next to it is a Lewis Hunter crane, bearing the number 3 on the cab side. *Associated British Ports*

To strengthen and support the dangerously high piles of pit props a method of stacking known as the 'birdcage' was used intermittently in the stacks, as seen here in the centre of the wood pile on the right in about 1932. *Associated British Ports*

This is hydraulic movable luffing crane No 26, one of many quayside cranes used in the docks that were operated by water under a pressure of 700 to 800 pounds per square inch. Each crane was capable of lifting, at a speed of 200 feet per minute, a load of 3 tons from 40 feet below quay level to 70 feet above quay level. No 26 was located in the timber yard in the north-west corner of Roath Dock. The LMS five-plank open wagon bears the number 315033, and its 18-inch lettering is in the 1920s style. It was photographed in 1932 against a background of sawn Scandinavian pit wood. The vessel on the extreme right is one of Guy's steam tugs, which operated in these docks for many years. *Associated British Ports*

On 3 August 1927 GWR locomotive No 6000 *King George V* is being loaded by the 70-ton crane aboard the vessel *Chicago City* at Roath Dock. The 'King' and the replica *North Star* – new and old locomotives – were to represent the Great Western Railway at the Baltimore & Ohio Railroad Centenary exhibition, which lasted from 24 September to 15 October 1927. *Associated British Ports*

In October 1927 *King George V* is back from its successful American tour, and the boiler is being carefully placed back on to the frames. *Associated British Ports*

It is May 1934 and this photograph shows a rake of LMS, GWR, and LNER ('NE') wooden open wagons at the north side of Roath Dock. The picture's original caption states that they are carrying milk for Europe, but that's open to debate! *Associated British Ports*

Again at the north side of the dock, Lewis Hunter movable luffing cranes (No 4 nearest the camera, with Nos 3, 2 and 1 behind) are loading hay from rail to ship from, in the centre, an LMS open 10-ton-tare wagon in about 1935. *Associated British Ports*

Iron Ore Wharf

As seen on the 1957 map, the north side of Roath Dock had been divided into two areas, a 'General Quay' and an 'Iron Ore Wharf'; the latter was later renamed 'GKN Iron Ore Wharf'. In 1982 it had become 'Dowlais Wharf', and by 1993 there was only two 10-ton grabbing crane in use at the wharf. Ten years later it was known as the EMR (European Metal Recycling) Scrap Berth, and is still in use today. Behind this scrap berth runs Roath Dock Road and the Eastern Bay Link Road, with the railway line that now supplies this side of Roath Dock with scrap metal for export running between them.

The wharf had its origin in the early part of the last century, when Messrs Guest, Keen & Nettlefolds Ltd rented 1,000 feet of wharf space in Roath Dock, where the company discharged its own vessels conveying iron ore from the continent to the huge Dowlais Works at Cardiff, which covered some 100 acres. The iron ore traffic was worked from the wharf to the works by means of a subway, and sometimes the ore taken in was brought out in the form of pig iron or steel plates within 48 hours, the latter being conveyed away by rail or ship to various shipbuilding or repairing yards. Steel rails or steel sleepers made at the company's Cyfarthfa Works, Merthyr Tydfil, were also loaded and dispatched from this wharf to India, Asia, and Africa.

In use at this wharf were 'Kangaroo' cranes, electrically operated cranes that were capable of handling a million tons of imported iron ore in a year. They lifted the ore from the vessels by means of giant octopus grabs, and it was then conveyed to the crushing plant and the steelworks stockyard by conveyor belts

Some of the ore came from Spain. *Ship Ahoy* magazine recorded in December 1963 that, 'The iron ore carrier *Trinculo* (1957, 11,206gt), bound for Cardiff, broke three main bearings and was completely disabled 75 miles off Vigo. She was … eventually brought from Vigo to Cardiff by the *Seefaake* (1924, 619gt)…' The same month 'The British motorship *Bannercliff* (1958, 7,490gt) loaded a record cargo of over 7,000 tons of wire rods from Guest, Keen & Nettlefolds Ltd, together with a number of cars and tractors, all destined for the Great Lakes ports.'

Loss of an iron ore cargo: from the *Pontypridd Chronicle*, 15 March 1884. *Pontypridd Library*

COLLISION AND SINKING OF A CARDIFF STEAMER.

Messrs. Hurley and Matthews, of Mount Stuart-square, Cardiff, received a brief telegram on Monday morning that their steamer William Griffiths (Captain Willmott) had been run into and sunk off Bilbao Bar, and that the crew were saved. The name of the colliding steamer is the Admiral Rooke, of Gibraltar. The William Griffiths was loaded with iron ore for Glasgow, and had left for that port on Saturday night.

In 1970 *Harbour Lights* magazine reported: 'A veteran to call at Cardiff was *Antonio De Satrustegui* (1920, 3,289gt). She arrived early in February, with iron ore from Spain.' Later in the year, 'Numerous iron ore carriers have been handled at Cardiff, due to Newport's closure, most of them regular callers to the Bristol Channel…'

Left Dowlais iron ore hopper wagons stand in front of Lewis Hunter hydraulic luffing cranes, which are loading rails aboard ship at Roath Dock in about 1905. *Associated British Ports*

Below Steel sleepers are being loaded aboard the SS *City of Christiania* at the Dowlais Iron Wharf in about 1926. Centre left is three-plank open wagon No 537, next to five-plank open No 036, both belonging to the GKN Company of Dowlais and showing two distinct styles of lettering. On the right is a 10-ton LNWR four-plank open wagon. The sleepers are probably bound for South Africa, where termites have a nasty habit of eating the wooden ones! *Associated British Ports*

Above This undated photograph shows hydraulic luffing cranes, probably of 6-ton lifting capacity, rigged for grabbing duties. These cranes were operated and maintained by the steelworks, and could be moved along the rails to suit the position of a ship's hold by turning hand gear that operated a geared winch. *Associated British Ports*

Below Another view of the GKN Iron Ore Wharf, this time in 1947, with a mixture of steel hopper wagons and former private owner colliery ten-plank open wagons, all being loaded with iron ore. *Associated British Ports*

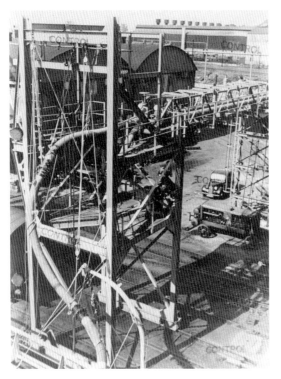

Left   This view of the Iron Ore Wharf taken on 19 September 1949 shows the overhead GKB oil pipeline; this carried its black liquid from ship to shore and onward into the GKN steelworks, which can be seen in the background. On the left is the corrugated-iron 'W' Warehouse. The steelwork dwarfs the stationary Austin car below. *Associated British Ports*

Below   Looking north-eastwards along the Iron Ore Wharf in about 1960, the rather magnificent structures are the electrically operated 'Kangaroo' cranes manufactured by Messrs Stothert & Pitt Ltd of Bath. The grab discharges its contents into a hopper built into the front of the crane, and the ore is then fed onto a conveyor to the rear of the wharf and carried into the works. These 'Kangaroo' cranes were only used at the Iron Ore Wharf (or berth, as it was later known). The first to be constructed, in position by June 1933, had a different type of grab. The vessel is the *Fairwater*, registered in Monrovia, Liberia. *Associated British Ports*

Above Another, more distant, view of the Iron Ore Wharf, circa 1960. The hopper under the driver's cab of the second crane can be seen, into which the grab would discharge its load. The worst problem was when the conveyor belts come off their drums, causing a pile-up of material; this would be announced by a loud siren and discharging of the vessel would cease until the men had dug out the ore and replaced the belt or put it back on the drum – very dirty work indeed. The cranes on the right are what remains of the original luffing cranes, seen in earlier photographs – some had been dismantled in April 1947. On the left are two partially built 'Kangaroo' cranes. Having her cargo discharged is the vessel *Laidaure*. *Associated British Ports*

Above right We can now see the eastern end of the conveyor system, which carried the iron ore from the quayside to the works. In July 1961 the ship at the berth is the *Cerro Bolivar*, fitted with twin kingposts at the forecastle, and seen with her steel cargo hatch covers open. *Associated British Ports*

Right The *Alexander T. Wood* is riding on 26 feet of water, and is in dire need of having her hull repainted. Her 13,500 tons of iron ore was the largest cargo to be discharged at the port, in February 1962. On the left, also at anchor but alongside the Grain Wharf, is the *Orecrest*, the shield on her bow reading 'Libertas'. The 'Kangaroo' cranes were dismantled in the 1990s by the Newport-based scrap metal firm of Messrs Ron Sheedy. *Associated British Ports*

Spillers Ltd

We have now reached the top of this dock, and on the north-eastern side, according to the 1901 map, was another large timber yard complex. On the 1904 map this part of Roath Dock was marked as yet another Import Wharf. A large circle of railway track surrounds this uppermost area of dockland, with a line leading from the nearby TVR storage sidings directly on to a long concrete jetty, built in 1887. This jetty was 800 feet long and 60 feet wide, and protruded from the centre of the Import Wharf into Roath Dock. At the centre of the jetty was a crane, alongside which was 'O' Warehouse, of stone construction with two floors; it measured 124 feet by 48 feet, and was used for the storage of sundry goods. Between this warehouse and the end of the jetty was a cold store, also known as 'O' Store; also of stone construction, it had three floors, measured 274ft 6in by 48 feet wide, and was used for the storage of perishable cargoes such as frozen meat. This cold store was demolished prior to the commencement of the building of Messrs Spillers mills and silo in 1932. Mooring posts were located on both sides of the jetty.

Later this wharf and jetty were to serve another purpose, for, as can be seen on the 1946 map, Spillers Ltd was by then located in the circle of track, with offices at one end, the silo at the other, and a warehouse in the middle. The silo was directly in line with the jetty and the grain conveyor.

By 1896 Cardiff was the fourth largest port in the United Kingdom, and was used for the importation of grain and flour. Premises were built and equipped at the West and East Bute Docks, but the increased size of grain-carrying steamers meant that vessels had to be discharged in the deep-water docks and the cargo transferred by barge to the grain wharves. A new site was therefore chosen at Roath Dock, where there was a water depth of 33ft 6in alongside the concrete jetty, and in 1932 Spillers' installation was ready for business, owned and operated by this well-known firm.

The silo was 230 feet long by 70 feet wide, and reached a height of 123 feet; it was capable of holding 30,000 tons of grain. To the left and behind the silo was the mill, with a capacity to produce 100 sacks of flour per hour. This also included a biscuit factory, while also on the left of the silo, but at the water's edge, was an animal food factory, then the warehousing and distribution centre, and over to the far left of the warehouse were the offices. Two pneumatic intake plants, travelling along the rails on the jetty, sucked the grain from the ships' holds into band conveyors, by

This is the newly built Spillers building with its silo and mills at Roath Dock, circa 1933, pictured in the GWR Ports booklet of 1937. On the right a vessel is berthed alongside the conveyor, which carries the grain along the wharf and into the mills. *Associated British Ports*

which it was transferred to the silo; the rate of discharge was from 200 to 250 tons per hour.

By 2003 all the buildings associated with this mill had gone, and today it is the site of 'E' Shed, while close by, also on land once occupied by the former Spillers group, is Marees Haulage Ltd. Beyond, located in the railway triangle above the dock, which was once North East Junction, near Clippers Place, is the timber complex of Britton's Timber Ltd.

Above The Grain Wharf was also known more accurately as the Grain Discharging Jetty, and this photograph shows the grain in the vessel's hold being unloaded by two suction elevators and going direct into the animal foodstuffs building in April 1947. These grain elevators unloaded grain at high speed, and could also sack, weigh and deposit grain into waiting barges alongside as an alternative to the grain elevator, when needed. *Associated British Ports*

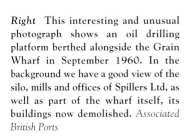

Right This interesting and unusual photograph shows an oil drilling platform berthed alongside the Grain Wharf in September 1960. In the background we have a good view of the silo, mills and offices of Spillers Ltd, as well as part of the wharf itself, its buildings now demolished. *Associated British Ports*

Floating cranes

Top The *GWR Magazine* of 1932 reported that 'the Company's 125-ton floating crane has been employed fairly regularly during the year at the principal South Wales docks. Besides being used on lifts by the Engineering Department and private contractors for repairing lock gates, erecting and transferring cranes, coaling hoists, and so on, the appliance was also been used for a number of important commercial shipments, including the placing of railway coaches on board ship.' This circa 1946 photograph shows the GWR's 100-ton floating crane being used to convey a railway coach, ordered by the Central Argentine Railway, from the quayside to a vessel for shipment to South America, assisted by two of the company's tugs. *Associated British Ports*

Middle Another floating crane, the *Simson III*, lifts a railway coach on to the deck of the *Barracoo* in about 1946. These floating cranes were steam driven, but needed the assistance of tugs to be manoeuvred into a position that enabled them to discharge their cargo. *Associated British Ports*

Bottom The GWR 100-ton floating crane is rendering assistance to the P. & A. Campbell paddle-steamer *Britannia* by placing a 48-ton oil-fired boiler in the stricken vessel on 1 July 1947. The new boiler was installed because her 'haystack' boiler, which dated from 1935, had partially collapsed while she was lying at the Pierhead, Cardiff, on the evening of 19 July 1946. *Associated British Ports*

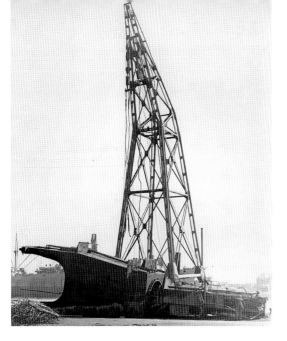

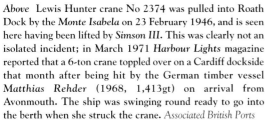

Above Lewis Hunter crane No 2374 was pulled into Roath Dock by the *Monte Isabela* on 23 February 1946, and is seen here having been lifted by *Simson III*. This was clearly not an isolated incident; in March 1971 *Harbour Lights* magazine reported that a 6-ton crane toppled over on a Cardiff dockside that month after being hit by the German timber vessel *Matthias Rehder* (1968, 1,413gt) on arrival from Avonmouth. The ship was swinging round ready to go into the berth when she struck the crane. *Associated British Ports*

Above right and below In June 1957 the 100-ton floating crane *Simson III* is lifting a 'stator' (which holds the windings that enclose the rotor part of the electric generator), built by Parsons Ltd, from the SS *Cromarty Firth* berthed alongside Spillers' Grain Wharf. It has possibly been ordered by the

Central Electricity Generating Board, and will be transported by road to the nearest power station in the area, at Rogerstone. Later the CEGB introduced its own specialised vessel and was able to bring these heavy units ashore without the assistance of cranes. The stator is being loaded on to a 24-wheeled low-loader with a 152-ton load capacity, just one of the many heavy haulage vehicles owned by Newport-based Wynns Ltd, this one built by the well-known firm of Cranes of Dereham. The puller driver is Bill Pitten and behind, inside the pusher, is driver Gill French. *Simson III*, complete with car tyres for fenders and that other piece of essential equipment, the bicycle, is being assisted by the British Transport Docks Board's tug *Cardiff*. This tug was purchased by Messrs R. & J. H. Rea Ltd on 14 July 1963, and by that Christmas had gone to the Newport yard of John Cashmore Ltd for scrap. *Associated British Ports*

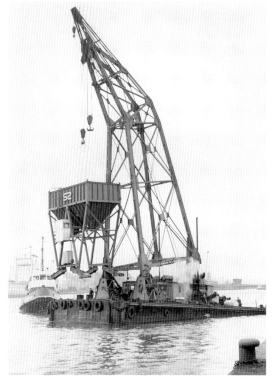

Above In August 1965, at the south side of Roath Dock, a heavy fabrication manufactured by Davidson & Co Ltd at the Sirocco Engineering Works, Belfast, is being lifted by a 50-ton floating crane; it has already lifted it out of the vessel in which it crossed the Irish Sea, and now suspends it while the driver, his mate and others prepare the bed of their trailer to receive the load for transportation to Aberthaw Power Station. The tug, *Exegarth*, will have assisted the crane to move around the dock – it looks as though part of this crane's equipment is also to have a pair of bicycles aboard! *Associated British Ports*

Left In about 1982 a top-loading, bottom-discharging hopper (quayside cranes would discharge into it while road or rail transport would load up under it) is being transported by the floating crane *Simson III* assisted by the tug *Danesgarth*. The hopper bears the new insignia of the British Transport Docks Board, which was introduced in 1982 when the docks came under the control of Associated British Ports; it has since been phased out and ABP's initials have taken its place. Note the 'Plimsoll line' painted onto the side of the crane's hull. This safety symbol was introduced after many years of campaigning by Samuel Plimsoll, when the Merchant Shipping Act was passed in 1876. However, in a compromise by Parliament, the load line could be placed anywhere the ship's owner wished. Finally, after more years of campaigning, it became legally enforced in 1894. Plimsoll well deserved his title 'The Sailors' Friend'. *Associated British Ports*

Oil and petroleum traffic

In the summer of 1962 *Ship Ahoy* magazine announced that

'On May 16th the MV *Tank Prince* (1950, 10,006gt) arrived at the Jet Petroleum Berth in the Roath Dock, Cardiff, from Rotterdam with the first cargo of oil for the new depot. In connection with the installation the BTC are to build a boom between Spiller's Jetty and the south side of the dock, thus completely enclosing the oil dock and minimising the risk of any fires spreading.'

Later the magazine announced that on 10 July the new Ocean Oil Terminal had been opened by the Lord Mayor of the city. 'The depot, which will supply petrol to Wales, the South Midlands, and the West of England, has a capacity for 20,000 tons, for three grades of petrol and also gas/diesel oil.'

The following year it was further reported that:

'Work is about to start soon on extensions that will more than double the present 20,000 tons capacity of the Jet Petroleum Company's £500,000 oil terminal at Roath Dock, Cardiff. The tanks are to be of larger capacity than the existing ones. The reason for the expansion is twofold: Jet want to accommodate at least 18,000-ton cargoes (at

present they can only take about 15,000 tons) and Conoco (UK), a subsidiary of Continental Oils, of which Jet is also a subsidiary, wish to distribute their brands of oil throughout South Wales, the Midlands, and the West Country.'

In December 1970 *Harbour Lights* magazine recorded:

'A new traffic which will figure in the trade returns for Cardiff from the end of this year will be bulk bitumen. A bitumen bulk storage tank farm, which would be capable of handling up to 150,000 tons a year, is being constructed alongside the Gulf Oil premises, Roath Dock.'

This traffic brought with it necessary facilities for cleaning out the oil tankers. Mr Bill Osborn, who worked for the Channel Dry Docks Company from 1939 until his retirement, provides details of tank-cleaning operations at the docks:

'At "Aberdan", as this "Oil Tanker Cleaning Installation" was called, oil tankers would be steam-cleaned and washed down. This was important so that the tanks would be gas-free before dry-docking. With these tankers, scale would form inside their tanks and gas would remain under it; this scale thus needed to be removed. Anodes were fitted inside the tanks

The Oil Tanker Cleaning Installation, on the north side of Roath Dock, is seen here on 13 August 1959. When legislation was first introduced banning ships from discharging their bilges of oily waste over the side, it became necessary to provide facilities for this purpose. Vessels were eventually equipped to deal with this waste and the need for the plant diminished, until it was finally made redundant. *Associated British Ports*

to counteract the chemical reaction with the oil, then, once the ship had dry-docked, a hole would be cut in the bottom of the tank and the scale was then pressure-hosed to the hole and onto the bottom of the dock. This was the easy way to remove it.'

Above Berthed at the Oil Tank Cleaning Installation, with the coal conveyor in the distance, is the Shell tanker *Naranio* and, behind her, the *Newcombia*, circa 1960. *Associated British Ports*

Below An aerial view of a tanker alongside the Cleaning Installation in about 1965. Nearby are the oil storage tanks of the Gulf and Conoco (UK) companies. *Associated British Ports*

Post-war developments

In the spring of 1963, *Ship Ahoy* reported that the longest vessel ever to dock at Roath Dock arrived at the beginning of February. She was the 658-foot-long Submarine Depot Ship HMS *Adamant* (15,000gt), and paid a six-day courtesy visit to the port with a complement of 750 officers and men.

The previous year a contract was placed for the construction of a new access road at Cardiff Docks, which would open up the area of land between Roath Dock and the foreshore, and would serve dock tenants in that area. In 1963 *Ship Ahoy* went on to report that 'By the end of 1964, the second stage, costing £200,000, of Rover Way, the Cardiff Docks Access Road, will be completed. It is hoped that the 24-feet carriageway will join the Roath Dock Road near the Jet Petroleum Tank Depot, and work is to start during September or October.'

By the end of the 1950s the railway lines that had once been so numerous on the south side of

the dock, were much reduced. The 1957 map shows only the two aforementioned coal conveyors, and one feeder road leading to the few remaining cranes. In the 1960s the ground was levelled for the stacking of imported timber, mainly from Scandinavia, Canada and the USA. Also by then more use was being made of road haulage facilities, and by the 1980s massive changes had taken place. At the end of Grain Wharf, reaching over to the south side, was the above-mentioned oil boom, which enclosed an area of water now known as the Oil Dock.

Not far from here was South East Junction and the Roath storage sidings, but by the 1980s the area of railway lines on the south side of the dock from the Communication Passage entrance to the oil boom had become known as Fletchers Wharves Ltd. Today the area is known as the General Cargo Wharf, and ABP's 2003 map shows erected on this ground a new building – Roath Dock Terminal, also known as 'H' Shed – near the Communications Passage entrance.

In this earlier view of the same wharf in about 1946, the belt conveyor is again seen in the distance, confirming this to be the south side of Roath Dock. Cased vehicles bound for Canada are being shipped aboard by 6-ton cranes. Under the legs of the loading crane are a pair of Vulcan road vehicles, tarpaulin sheets on top of their cabs, while an internal-user railway wagon in the middle distance bears the serial number GW 204479. The 'Liberty' ship still has her wartime life rafts at the ready, and her funnel type indicates that she is one of the Canadian-built 'Fort' or 'Parks' Class built on orders from the Ministry of War. *Associated British Ports*

Left In March 1955 the tanker *Laristan* is at berth at the former Pontoon Wharf, photographed from the Inner Lock entrance at Roath Dock. She was one of the vessels owned by the Hindustan SS Company Ltd. *Associated British Ports*

Above This panoramic view from November 1957 shows the storage sidings on the south side of Roath Dock. In the middle distance on the left is a tall building next to some coal heaps: this is all that remains of the former Coal Washery. In the far distance is Spillers' Grain Mills, and on the far side of Roath Dock can be seen the cranes along Iron Ore Wharf.

On the right is a large expanse of ground known as the 'Prairie', and it was on this desolate site that equipment, vehicles, artillery guns and soldiers were stationed during the Second World War. Another eight years were to pass before this area was levelled and coal would give way to the import of timber. *Associated British Ports*

Left By about 1965 work in under way to clear the site. The Coal Washery building survives, awaiting demolition, and the new oil tanks on the extreme right are part of the Gulf Oil tank storage depot. The buildings in the foreground were occupied by the docks' relocated tenants, among them Messrs Fletchers Ltd timber importers, until they built new premises. Compass Road can be seen heading towards the oil tanks, with Cold Store Road nearest the camera. *Associated British Ports*

This interior view of 'N' Shed, on the north side of Roath Dock, shows the first floor, which was used for general goods, on 22 January 1957. The barrels of tobacco have been discharged from the *Manchester Merchant*, and carry various markings: enclosed in the diamonds are such inscriptions as 'CD 2 leaf 1956', 'CG leaf 1956', 'CD leaf 1956' and 'PG leaf 1956'. All of this cargo is en route to the Imperial Tobacco Company of Great Britain Ltd. *Associated British Ports*

Motor cars for export in May 1960: arriving by rail are a line of Triumph TR3A soft-top sports cars, and behind them are Vauxhall Victor F series cars. Temporarily held at the sidings on the south side of Roath Dock Basin, near Communications Passage, they will soon be lifted from these British Railways 13-ton 'Carfit-S' trucks. Later this area became part of Fletchers Ltd. The large building in the middle distance has the words 'James Arnett & Sons Ltd' painted on its roof. *Associated British Ports*

This September 1960 shipment of Ford Anglia 105E deluxe motor cars is also destined for abroad – all have left-hand drive. The GKN steelworks can be seen in the distance. *Associated British Ports*

In February 1960 Army tanks are being discharged from the *Benalbanach*, of Leith, Scotland. Each tank carries on its side its ship embarkation number; in the upper picture it is 'F.S.O.T.A./8090'. This Centurion, being steadied on its sling before being finally lowered into place by the ship's gantry crane onto the tank transporter, has been named 'Flying Bronco', a tradition that goes back to 1916; its road registration number is 08ZR48. The second picture shows the squadron of Centurions lined up and preparing to leave Roath Dock; they and their crews have returned from abroad, but they still have to complete the journey to their home garrison. *Associated British Ports*

Right This December 1960 photograph shows the framework of an oil rig being unloaded by the ship's derrick. Beside the second section in the background are vehicles belonging to Wynn's heavy haulage company: the nearest is an AEC, and behind it a Scammell.

Below In October 1960 MV *City of Poona* discharges crushed bones to road and rail vehicles, and over the side to the coastal vessel *Sprayville*, which was one of a number of British coasters operated and owned by Messrs John S. Monks Ltd, of Liverpool.

In the summer of 1968 *Ship Ahoy* magazine recorded that, 'Following a case of anthrax in a docker unloading crushed bone from India some months ago, new facilities for unloading the bone involving minimal handling have been installed at the Roath Dock, Cardiff, opposite Fletchers Timber Wharf. As yet no ships have berthed at this wharf.'

The autumn edition added: 'A pneumatic plant for the discharge of crushed bones has been installed at Cardiff Docks. The bone is used in the production of gelatine by P. Leiner & Sons at their Treforest factory; it is an occasional source of anthrax infection and the suction plant which deposits the bone from the ship's hold into storage bins has been introduced to cut down the risk of infecting dockers. The first ship to use the new plant was the *City of Ottawa* (1950, 7,622gt), which arrived on 19 June and discharged 1,200 tons of crushed bone from India and Pakistan.' *Associated British Ports*

Left A close view of Leiner's bone suction plant in May 1968. In the background, seen through the legs of dockside crane No 43, Spillers' mill can be seen, especially the animal foodstuffs plant at the water's edge. *Associated British Ports*

Below In June 1968 another vessel with a cargo of crushed bone, its steel cargo hold covers open, is ready to discharge into Leiner's bone suction plant on the left (on the site of the by now demolished 'N' and 'W' Warehouses). In the middle distance can be seen the overhead oil pipe supplying fuel to the nearby GKN steelworks, and further down the dock is the Iron Ore Wharf, its 'Kangaroo' cranes busy discharging scrap metal from the berthed vessel *Cape Franklin* direct to the conveyor belt beneath them, which carries it directly to the crushing plant. On the extreme right, berthed alongside the offices of Spillers' Grain Mill, is the vessel *Oste*. *Associated British Ports*

Above A transformer for Cilfynydd has been offloaded at Roath Dock in June 1968, and mounted on a Cranes of Dereham 48-wheel Swan trailer, of 300-ton capacity, with bogies at each end (Fleet No 789). Two Scammell tractors were used with this contract, one in front as a puller and the other a pusher at the rear. The puller driver was Tommy Cromwell and the pusher driver Albert Vincent, experienced drivers for the heavy haulage firm of Wynns Ltd. Behind the trailer is a Commer, the 'ACE' (Air Cushion Equipment) vehicle, equipped with a two-stroke pump that was able to relieve one-third of the weight of the trailer's two bogies. *Associated British Ports*

Below Taken in 1973, this photograph shows the aftermath of the work undertaken some eight years earlier whereby, to accommodate a new bulk timber import contract, the sheds seen here were erected, and the rest of the ground area levelled for use as open timber storage. The Gulf tank storage farm is close by, and helps to confirm that this area is the south side of Roath Dock. These sheds would later on be known as 'H' Shed. The Russian vessel nearest the camera is the *Yevgnee Nikdnov. Associated British Ports*

Above This is Ryan's coal blending site on the north side of Roath Dock in September 1984. In the background can be seen the ventilators of the Rod Mill. This storage area was formerly known as Pontoon Wharf, and Ryan's used it to stockpile cargoes of imported coal, primary for use in Aberthaw Power Station. In 1991 the site was closed, although a new coal-blending site was opened on the south side of the dock, and subsequently part of the north side was used by the CGB of Didcot, and is now used for the storage of barrage construction materials by Balfour Beatty Costain Ltd. *Author*

Below In this second view from the former Pontoon Wharf, on 6 March 1987, the vessel berthed alongside the former Dowlais Wharf unloading its cargo of scrap iron via an octopus grab is the *Tirgubujor*. On the right is the Grain Jetty, at the top of which is Spillers' Grain Mill and silo; alongside can be seen a long low building, which is a custom-built silo for animal foodstuffs, built to cater for a specific import contract. *Author*

Right In October 1987 Class 08 diesel shunter No 08818 crosses over Clipper Road level crossing, on the south side of Roath Dock, parallel to the side of Spillers' Grain Mill. *Author*

Below right Two more Class 08s are seen here, No 08796 on the right and No 08654 on the left, photographed at 12.40pm on 11 February 1987. They are standing by the permanent way and rest hut alongside Roath Dock Road on the north side of the dock. Behind the camera is Ryan's coal-blending dump. *Author*

Below At Tidal Sidings on 14 February 1987 these two Class 08s, No 08461 (right) and No 08804, are alongside the former ASW Tremorfa Works, which later became part of the Celsa Steel Group. Between this building and the diesel engines are a number of empty British Railways 21-ton steel-sided mineral wagons; 1,500 of these were built in 1950/51 for domestic coal traffic and they were also used on a large scale for supplying coal to power stations and large works. *Author*

Left Again at Tidal Sidings, alongside the Tremorfa Steelworks, are Nos 08654 (right) and 08818 at 5.30pm on 6 March 1987. *Author*

Left This is North East Junction signal box, a GWR-designed structure that replaced the earlier Cardiff Railway Company box. Still in place on 27 March 1987, it stood near Clipper Road and Roath Dock Road; looking towards the ASW Rod Mill (Castle Works) can be seen gantries that once held semaphore railway signals. *Author*

Below Another view of North East Junction signal box on the same day, this time looking towards the ASW Tremorfa Works, with diesel No 08654 in view. On the right is Webb's timber yard. The signal box was eventually destroyed by fire. *Author*

In this panoramic view from Lewis Road, the line on the left heads towards the south side of Roath Dock and beyond, while that on the right heads towards North East Junction signal box and onwards to the Rod Mill's Castle Works. Between the branches can be seen Webb's timber yard, and between the yard and the signal box is ASW diesel loco No 372 hauling a rake of wire coils in October 1987. The second picture shows the No 372 about to pass underneath the Lewis Road bridge. *Author*

ORDNANCE SURVEY REFERENCES

The following National Grid references cover the main locations around the Bute and Roath Docks, some of which, due to modern development, have been lost for ever, while others are situated around and inside the present-day Port of Cardiff.

Bute West Dock
    Basin, Outer Lock entrance   ST193744-(untraceable)
    Basin, Inner Lock entrance   ST194746-(untraceable)
    Dock, west side   ST193746-ST189757
    Dock, east side   ST193747-ST 190757
    Pierhead Building   ST193744

Bute East Dock
    Basin, Outer Lock entrance   ST193744-ST194747
    Basin, Inner Lock entrance   ST194746-ST195747
    Basin   ST193745-ST194746
    Dock, west side   ST194747-ST191758
    Dock, east side   ST195747-ST192759
Dowlais Steel Works (later GKN)   ST196760-ST197751,
                                      ST199762-ST203751
Cardiff Rod Mill, Castle Works   ST199749-ST194759
Junction Lock (East Dock to Roath Basin)   ST195747-ST196745

Roath Dock
    Basin, Outer Lock entrance   ST194742-ST195743
    Basin, Inner Lock   ST198745-ST197746
    Basin, north side   ST195547-ST197746
    Basin, south side   ST195742-ST198744
    Dock, north side   ST199747-ST205742
    Dock, south side   ST200745-ST206750
Bute Dry Dock   ST195742-ST195736
Channel Dry Dock   ST194738-ST195740
Commercial Dry Dock   ST197746-ST195741
GWR Engineering Workshops   ST197745
Cattle lairs   ST198746
Crown Fuel Works   ST199745
Communication Passage (Roath Dock side) ST200746-ST201742
Communication Passage swingbridge   ST200746
Spillers Grain Wharf   ST203749-ST205741
Roath Storage Sidings   ST208752-ST209754
Roath Tidal Sidings   ST209756-ST206763
Tremorfa Steelworks (Celsa UK Ltd)   ST209759-ST208762,
                                    ST211761-ST20763

ACKNOWLEDGEMENTS

I would like to thank the following for their help with these books:

Dr Don Anderson, Roath, Cardiff (former editor of *Ship Ahoy* magazine); Associated British Ports, Cardiff; Birmingham Central Library; Ian Bolton, Social Sciences Department, Birmingham Central Library; Brenda Brownjohn, *The Railway Magazine*, London; L. D. Bryant, Pencoed, Mid Glamorgan; Sarah Canham, Research Centre Assistant, National Railway Museum, York; R. S. Carpenter, Hollywood, Birmingham; Richard M. Casserley, Berkhamsted; Andrew Choong, Curator, National Maritime Museum, Greenwich, London; Stephen Cole, Local Studies Department, Cardiff Central Library; Chris Collard, Rumney, Cardiff (former editor of *Ship Ahoy* magazine); Katrina Coopey, Local Studies Department, Cardiff Central Library; Callum Couper, Port Manager, Associated British Ports, Cardiff; Michael Crabb, Easton, Portland, Dorset; Viv Crabb, Pontypridd, Mid Glamorgan; John Curle, Wyke Regis, Dorset; Ted Darke, Easton, Portland, Dorset; Martyn Farquhar, Portland, Dorset; Fleet Air Arm Museum, Yeovilton, Somerset; David Fletcher, Curator, Tank Museum, Bovington, Dorset; John Fry, Ely, Cardiff; J. and J Collection, c/o D. K. Jones, Mountain Ash, Mid Glamorgan; Brian Gambles, Birmingham Central Library; Stuart Hadaway, Assistant Curator, Department of Research & Information, RAF Museum; Michael Hale, Woodsetton, Dudley; *Harbour Lights* magazine, Swansea; Cliff W. Harris, Porth, Mid Glamorgan; John Hodge, Haywards Heath, W Sussex; Frank Hornby, Sutton, Surrey; *Illustrated London News* Picture Library; Cliff C. James, Taffs Well, Mid Glamorgan; Mike Jarvis, Civil Engineer's Department, Associated British Ports, Cardiff; David Jenkins, Curator, National Waterfront Museum, Swansea; Derek K. Jones, Mountain Ash, Mid Glamorgan; Glyndwr G. Jones, Bromley, Kent; Mrs Jan Keohane, Archivist, Fleet Air Arm Museum, Yeovilton, Somerset; Lens of Sutton Association; Harold Lloyd, Sully, Vale of Glamorgan; Locomotive Club of Great Britain (Ken Nunn Collection); Doreen Luff, Cardiff; Tony Luff, Portland, Dorset; Keith Luxton, Taffs Well, Mid Glamorgan; Hywel Mathews, Pontypridd Library; Mrs L. Morris, Area Librarian, Pontypridd Library; National Railway Museum, York; Ordnance Survey Department, Southampton; John O'Brien, Pentwyn, Cardiff; Bill Osborn, Penarth, South Glamorgan; George Pearce, Grangetown, Cardiff; *Pontypridd and Llantrisant Observer*; Pontypridd Library, Mid Glamorgan; Alun G. Powell, Rhydyfelin, Pontypridd, Mid Glamorgan; Royal Air Force Museum, London; *The Railway Magazine*, London; Doug Richards, Pencoed, Mid Glamorgan; Keith Robbins, GWS, Didcot, Oxfordshire; *Ship Ahoy* magazine, Cardiff, South Glamorgan; Graham Stacey, LCGB, Egham, Surrey; Brian Stephenson, RAS Marketing, Ashford, Kent; Clive Thomas, Deputy Port Manager, Associated British Ports, Cardiff; R. E. Toop, Bath; Mrs Elaine Tuft, Trowbridge, Cardiff; John Wynn (retired), Wynn's (Heavy Haulage) Ltd, Newport, Gwent; Peter Wynn, Wynn's (Heavy Haulage) Ltd, Eccleshall, Staffordshire.

I would like to give a special mention to Mrs Hillary Lloyd Fernandez, who after many years of service has now retired from Associated British Ports, Cardiff, and at present is enjoying a well-earned holiday with her husband Andrew and their son Alexander.

Associated British Ports, Cardiff, and their staff have always shown great hospitality to me during my many visits to them over the years, during which time two former members of staff have passed away. I would therefore like to offer my condolences to the widows of John B. Phelps and Norman Watts; both were true gentlemen and it was an honour to have known them.

INDEX